BEAUTY
BEYOND THE SCARS

A Second Chance at Life… A Second Chance at Love

By

Zelda D. Johnson

Copyright © 2024 Zelda D. Johnson

All rights reserved. No part of this publication may be reproduced, distributed, or transmitted in any form or by any means, including photocopying, recording, or other electronic or mechanical methods, without the prior written permission of the publisher, except in the case of brief quotations embodied in critical reviews and certain other noncommercial uses permitted by copyright law. For permission requests, write to the publisher, addressed "Attention: Permissions Coordinator," at the address below.

ISBN: (Paperback) 979-8-9891901-2-6

I have tried to recreate events, locales, and conversations from my memories of them. I may have changed some identifying characteristics, and details such as physical properties, occupations, and places of residence. You will also observe me straying at times from the storyline here and there; just to address some of life's questions while writing this book. I am sharing just a few of "life's nuggets if you will. Additionally, a few of my close family, and friends answered some questions regarding their experiences in relation to me and my journey.

Editors
Teresa Hamilton
Doc Wilson

Publisher
Imagination Press, LLC
101 Cherry Lane
Glen Burnie, Maryland 21060

First printing edition 2024

www.imaginationpress.website

TABLE OF CONTENTS

Dedication 5
Introduction 6
Chapter 1: A Family Affair 8
    Baltimore's Finest 8
    Only a Heart Knows for Sure 9
    My Mom - The Caring Creator 10
    My Dad – The Unique Charismatic Preacher ... 12
    Siblings 101 – My Guardian Angels 15
    What Did You Say I Could Be? 19
    Hopes, Dreams and Fears, Oh My! 22
    Love Connections 23
    Trusting God and Yourself – The True Connection ... 27
    A Fork in the Road – Me, Myself, and I 31
    Working to Find My Way 31
    Entrepreneurship and Being An Author 33
    Growing up Mentally – What You See Is What You… ... 34

Chapter 2: Exploring Beautiful Relationships Love and Marriage and Everything in Between ... 36
    Beginning of the End – The Wonder Years 39
    My Happily Ever After: Adrian S. Johnson 41
    Never Knew Love Like This Before 47
    A True Second Chance 51

Chapter 3: Beauty Interrupted Surviving My Second Quarantine ... 53
    Close Encounters of a Scary Time 68
    Family and Friends In Their Own Words From the Heart Give an Account of My Illness ... 70

Chapter 4: Beautiful Words of Wisdom 89
    Secrets to a successful marriage 89

Dealing with Adversity – A Game Changer ... 92
Parents and Communities: Let's Work Together ... 94
Community Relationships – No Man is an Island ... 97
A New Outlook – Health is Wealth ... 98
Rededicating Our Lives to Christ ... 105
The End…Or Just The Beginning ... 106
MY FAMILY ALBUM ... 112
Old Friends - Adrian & Zelda Our Happily Ever After ... 113
The Lanes Sugar and Spice ... 114
My FAMILY ... 115
Cousin Connections First and Second Cousins ... 116
The Brother's Johnson with their mom and dad ... 117
Friends Who Became Family The Walls, The Bentleys, and The Johnsons ... 118
SUGGESTED READINGS ... 121
SPEAKING ENGAGEMENTS AND BOOKINGS ... 122
THE A2Z EXPERIENCE ... 123
DEDICATED ORGANIZATIONS ... 124
BIBLICAL SCRIPTURES ... 126
AFFIRMATIONS FROM THE HEART! ... 128

DEDICATION

To my mom, Lorraine Beatrice Richardson Lane who was a beautiful woman on the outside and a more lovely person on the inside.

You gave birth to me at thirty-six years old. I was your surprise baby! I so loved you as you loved me. You were my "Shero," before I even knew the term. Thank you for being my girl by simply doing what mother's do.

Whether you were near or far, just hearing your voice talking or singing a song soothed my little soul until I became an adult. My heart, my soul, and my spirit will forever be grateful for God placing us together as mother and daughter. I miss you deeply but often times feel your presence with me. Until next time mom. Keep smiling, singing, and shining your heavenly spirit down from heaven.

Today, I graciously give thanks to Almighty God, and everyone who has been connected to me, as part of my life's journey.

INTRODUCTION

Trauma, Who Knows Trauma? A black girl born in the sixties, in the midst of the civil rights era. I was the youngest child. Some would say, I was a crazy but modest teenager, a single mom, a young wife, and a divorcee. I reconnected to love again, and experienced heart health challenges twice (six surgeries in total). I chose to live life with many life lessons learned. Loving life in spite of a few regrets, as well as a few do overs. I have learned to just be me while going from trauma to triumph!

I would like to start with this. Even if your plans may have changed along the way. Due to your intent or with no plans of your own. Always remember this...God says, "For I Know The Plans I Have For You Declares The Lord. Plans To Prosper You And Not Harm You, Plans To Give You Hope And A Future." Jeremiah 29:11 You may have gone through your own personal traumas in life, but you can come out on top too. Trauma in your life, whatever that may look like for you. It really is up to you to be intentional about your life. How you live it, and respond to it. The song rings true, "We fall down but we get up." You must choose to get up and WIN! I'm telling you right now. Hey, wait, did I say it would always be easy? Success is success no matter how big or how small. We must learn to celebrate them all; that Future, which was mentioned in Jeremiah. Well, you and I were created to help create our futures. Let's dive in as I share, a little piece of me and a whole lot of God!

Chapter 1

A Family Affair

Baltimore's Finest

I was born in Baltimore, Maryland on December 14, 1963, at Johns Hopkins Hospital. I was told prior to my parents moving to Baltimore (before my birth) that they had lived in several different states; Virginia, North Carolina, and New Orleans. Just think I could have been a bayou baby because my parents moved around so much. Baltimore was where I started my life's journey, until the age of 18 after high school, then I moved to Richmond, Virginia. I was missing my family and friends and also the land that I love. OK, no I didn't join the military or explore the jungles of Africa, or climb Mount Everest. Well, let's just see where the story goes.

Only a Heart Knows for Sure

My father Morris R. Lane was a minister, and my mother Lorraine B. Lane was a First Lady. I was born into Christianity from day one. My parents met in Halifax County, Virginia. Both of them met while attending Halifax High School and lived in South Boston, Virginia. It was love at first sight; okay let me stop. Well, I did hear that my dad said that my mom was going to be the one. He had several people praying for him in regard to his marriage to my mother. One of my mom's sisters didn't care for him because she thought of him as a gigolo, or a player back then. You know, fresh with the ladies. However, as far as my dad was concerned, prayer changes things. Can I get an Amen? I am here aren't I? You Go God!

My Mom - The Caring Creator

My mom was a beautiful light complexion woman, who I thought had the most beautiful light-colored eyes and beautiful hair. Most of all, her infectious delightful spirit would always shine through. She loved to laugh which she passed down to her children until this day. My mom, being the baby of her family of six siblings (four girls and two boys) traveled very often to visit her siblings in Richmond, Virginia, Newark, New Jersey, Greensboro, North Carolina, and Portsmouth and Clarksville, Virginia. There was my Aunt Lesty Ann known as "Honey" and just as sweet, my Aunt Mable, our prayer warrior, Uncle John, sturdy but calm, Uncle Garnett just smooth and her oldest sister, my Aunt Viola. I just remember when I was a child making my Aunt Viola laugh.

My mom was very close to her niece, Mary as well. Being close in age, they grew up together like sisters. She would also visit with Mary when she would visit New Jersey to see my Aunt Mable and Uncle Wagner. I thank and honor all of them for the role they played in my life. She traveled very often to see her siblings in Richmond, Virginia and Newark, New Jersey. She was the one sibling to always visit all of her sisters and brothers. Because I was the youngest of my family, I had the privilege of going along for the ride during my summer vacations and on holidays. It became a holiday and vacation tradition with my mother. My mom as I always remembered was a delight to be around. My mom was a hairdresser and had similar interests in cosmetology. I became a cosmetologist myself. I didn't know that I had the same skill set until my teenage years. My mother liked to sew, and she was also a seamstress for several companies.

She worked at a shoe factory in her early years, and she was a seamstress making men's suits in Towson, Maryland. She then went on to start creating something she had a love for; making and designing hats especially fancy church lady hats. The name of her business was "Heavenly Creations." As stated before, she became a preacher's wife and the First Lady of several churches, and my dad became the Pastor, and he was affiliated with several denominations. She also taught herself how to play the piano which she played in most church services.

Traveling to several different places as a young adult with my family; I realized that my dad was a career pastor. Who knew! So, my mom's fascination with hats and designing them became a passion of hers. She started to create several hats which eventually resulted in her becoming an entrepreneur, and owning her own business after her job closed down while she was on vacation without notice. A day I will never forget. She learned from the news that she no longer had a job while watching the evening news. Chains and very large locks were placed on fences around the building with no access in the building. I remember riding with her, and discovering that the clothing factory she worked for was no longer in business. Little did she know that the closure of her job would lead her to fully embrace entrepreneurship. Wow! You never know how when one door closes; God can open a window. In her adversity, my mom discovered that creating hats on her own was truly her passion and ultimately her blessing.

I am finding over time just how much my mom and I had in common and were similar in a lot of ways. My mom, just like any of our moms, could fill up many pages just talking about her. Her love and loyalty toward her husband of over fifty plus years was challenging and amazing. She also had a wonderful connection with each of her children, her extended family, and friends who became family. My mom was good with strangers… she had that "Je ne sais quoi" That song will always be in my heart, *I'll Always Love My Mama, She's My Favorite Girl.* No one like her. Thank you God for placing me with her. *What a Woman, What a Woman, What a Mighty Good Woman.* This song describes my mom in a nutshell.

My Dad – The Unique Charismatic Preacher

Now my dad on the other hand, just kidding. You do sometimes understand a person much better after they are no longer with you. My dad was my dad. He was an only child and all that comes with that. I found that we all act in our adult years the way we were brought up, shaped, and molded in our younger years. It's something that you can't go back and change or ask for a do-over. As the saying goes, "It is what it is." However, I do believe we have the power each new day to change the direction of our lives if we chose to do so. We all do live, and we learn.

I look back at my dad and from what I've come to learn; he learned some hard lessons in life. Some lessons were necessary, and some I am sure were not. For my mom, she had five other siblings and two parents to lean on. He never had that love and support of others constantly around him. My dad's parents split up when he was a baby living in New York, and he was an only child, which made it more of a challenge for him. He was the oldest, middle, and the youngest child all at once. Well, maybe not middle but you get the point. My grandmother (Marie Jones), after her divorce became a single parent for many years until she remarried after leaving an abusive relationship with my grandfather who I never met. He chose not to come back from New York to Virginia because she had some nice but unhappy brothers who dared him to come back to Virginia. Ok, enough said! Mr. Harvey, who became my step grandfather, often worked away from home (as an underground pipe layer) but always sent her money to take care of things. Just FYI, once he had me take a puff on a cigarette, I was around seven or eight. It choked me to death; he just laughed. I guess that is why I never smoked. Go figure!

My Grandma Gee Gee (paternal grandmother), as we called her would often come to visit us from Virginia for months at a time during the winter months in Maryland. She cooked wonderful meals, and would take and pick me up from school. During the summer months, I would stay with her for a while, then she would escort me to spend time with my mom's parents. Lectherd and Gela Richardson were my other set of grandparents who lived in the same little town about 5 miles away from her.

My dad worked for a Phillip Morris factory in Virginia during his early years. He also worked in an emergency room at a local hospital, while becoming a minister, teacher, and preacher of the Faith. My dad was a tall man, at least 6'2". Always dressed in a suit, shirt, tie, and slacks and oh let's not forget the hats. He never stuck his head out the door without a hat. He was somewhat of a stylish man. I never saw my dad in a pair of overhaul jeans until I was married and in my twenties. Not only wearing his suits, and Hamburg hats (never a baseball or leisure cap of any kind). My dad would have several of his robes custom made, and he would even help design them. He would preach in these robes during church service, and on special occasions. Now, I get it. Style and design is everything. No, not really. Well, all I know is both my parents had it, so I guess that's why I tried to emulate them the best I can!

BEAUTY BEYOND THE SCARS

Also, I can remember riding in the car, and it was so hot at times; I just could not breathe. Ok, just me being me. It felt like I couldn't breathe. I later learned the reasons my dad didn't go without a hat was that he was prone to catching bad colds very easily and he also did not care for air conditioners. That's why he wanted to keep his head covered, and we could barely breath in the summertime with the windows cracked in the car. Sometimes you don't know what you don't know. Oh yeah, and he was a country boy too, and he loved the fresh air.

All in all, my dad was someone who I loved and admired. As the baby of the group, my older siblings always felt that my parents were tired and just didn't have the energy they once had. So they allowed the younger sibling (me) to get away with so much more than the older siblings were able to get away with during their younger years. This is what I've been told. They have stories that I don't have and sometimes different experiences. I felt I could talk to my dad. I feared him of course, but I was never too afraid to ask for what I wanted. It took him quite some time to say why or why not I could or could not have something that I wanted. But in most of the cases, it was in my favor. Won't he do it!

I chose to do what he always preached and taught when it comes down to even our relationship. Looking back., he always said, "Eat The Fish But Spit Out The Bones." That is a constant staple in my life today. Only take what applies to you, and leave the rest alone. Last but not least, he taught me faith. I think more directly as well as indirectly. Through hearing his sermons over and over again, my dad was known as "The Book, Chapter, and Verse" preacher. He could tap his finger on his head while preaching and scriptures would just flow out of him effortlessly. He could do this because of the memory, and the mind he had. Along with the countless hours he would study God's Word. Along with the Bible, I saw many different books across his bed that he would use to study. Many of these books were donated to one of my dad's spiritual sons in ministry after my dad's passing. He also had some very unusual topics. There were so many. I want to just highlight one in particular. "I Have Seen Something That God Hasn't Seen!" Love you Dad. Oh, you're waiting to hear. Catch me a little later at the end. I believe you have too. I know preacher's kids over the years always seem to get a bad reputation as being worse than anyone else. Overall, I found we were human just like everybody else. We had the same struggles and challenges. We were never meant to be superhumans. Our lives were just more magnified than the other kids. So to all my PK's out there, much love to you. We survived!!!

Siblings 101 – My Guardian Angels

What can I say about my siblings? They shielded, protected, took care of me, and loved me. All three in their own way. Remember, I told you I was the baby right. I could not have asked for a better family. What I think did it for us even until this day is laughter. No matter what, we laughed our way through life. I know that may sound strange. We all have been told we have the best and most contagious smiles. Even though there has been some pain and some rain. We have always had each other. We may have had to cry through to get to the other side, but we managed to end up many times laughing so hard that we ended up crying. I have three siblings. Two sisters, Belinda, and Diana. Along with one brother Donnal who is deceased and extremely missed.

Belinda

My oldest sister Belinda left home at an early age but would always come and pick me up. She would take me to different places like the Ringling Bros. Circus, Holiday On Ice or just to her apartment to hang out. I always would get excited every time I knew she was coming, and I would spend some time with her. We are 13 years apart but sometimes I think we probably could have been twins. She has been a staple, a compass, and continuous cheerleader in my life. Our hearts and minds will forever be joined together. Our thought process is so much alike. We have traveled together, lived together, and always laughed together. The kind of laughter where you cannot stop or help yourself from laughing. I remember singing to the tiptop of my voice listening to her album collection (Natalie Cole and Tramaine Hawkins) at her townhouse apartment in Freedom Way Apartments in Baltimore, Maryland. I also remember being snowed in at her house and not being able to attend school for over a week. Ahhh, the good old days. Even the unspoken words, just knowing what the other was thinking. She is not only my sister, but she became my mother figure, when we lost our mother in 2007. Belinda has been my confidant, and one of my dearest best friends.

Diana

My other sister Diana and I spent more time together in my early years. She helped me tell time and tie my shoes. We actually shared a room together. She was 12 years older than me. I remember her working and purchasing her first color television for our room. Now that was fun. We also sang in the choir together, and went on many trips together. She was in the delivery room with me at the birth of my first daughter, Crystal. I was scared to death. She was with me every step of the way throughout my pregnancy as well. When she got married, I cried like a baby because I wanted to go on their honeymoon with her. Okay, I was 12, and my best friend was leaving me to go to Atlantic City. That sounds exciting, right? Remember we traveled together. Not to mention, I loved my new brother-in-law Clarence too.

Diana, my prayer warrior of the family. You better get you one. If you don't have one, sorry, you can't have mine. Ok, just kidding. She will pray for any, and everyone in whatever situation. She's my beautiful soul.

As time went on my sister Diana, and her husband Clarence had four children (Rochel, Eric, Derrick, and Terrance). I was the big auntie even though I was about twelve. I would often go with her to get their shots and checkups at the doctors' office. You would have thought the doctor was giving me the shots. I wanted to cry with them. Now as far as my brother-in-law who became one of my other brothers, he was so funny and he could cook anytime of the night or day, WOW! If you came to see them, as soon as you came in the door, he was in the kitchen cooking, and you would have a meal before you left. Boy, he was fast. How did he do that? He always made you laugh or smile. I used to call him Billy Dee Williams because he was usually dressed so sharp. He laughed and told me to, "Stop, Stop, Stop, Zelda," and then he would egg me on to continue saying it underneath his breath. Boy, have I missed him. He has been gone since 1999 but not forgotten.

Donnal

Now as far as my big brother Donnal is concerned, what can I say, and where do I start. He too was a combination of my mom and my dad. He was sweet and would do anything for you just like my mom. However, he could be stubborn like my dad at times. My parents wanted a boy and once he came of course they thought they were finished; well as Gomer Pyle would say, "Surprise, surprise, surprise," and here I come. I loved watching that show with my dad. My brother always looked out for me, as he did all three of his sisters. He was my ride or die or should I say my ride and let's live because we had a ball. He always kept us laughing and he was that type of guy that if you saw him over in the corner with someone usually his shoulders were going up and down, and the person was probably bent over laughing. He would literally give you his last, and the shirt off his back or should I say pull money straight out of his front shirt pocket if you were ever in need. He was like a human ATM. OK, was that just me? No! As we all know he was like that with everyone. He was my "ride or die" and my financier. So glad to have known him. He was truly my first best friend.

> **This is just an excerpt from one of my adopted brothers Clayton Jones's book.** *Who Else Could It Be but God?*
>
> Clayton Jones is one of my adopted brothers who was a good friend of my brother, Donnal.
>
> "Donnal who else could it be but God? Clayton wrote an entire chapter about his relationship and the impact that my brother had on his life. It has brought me to tears each time I have read it, and I quote. "When I looked at Donnal for the first time, he was average. I'm very happy to say that it's through Donnal that I was able to see a true example of an above average person."

For all of those that knew him, those words stand true. Sometimes you only get to meet a few above average people in our lifetime, and my brother was one of them.

I miss him with an everlastingness miss (if there's such a thing). So glad to have known him and to have had him in my life. I will always feel Donnal's presence cheering me on from above. My big brother; we really don't know if we will truly know each other in eternity, but I hope and pray we will all laugh together again one day. Along my life's journey, I have been fortunate to have not blood, but several brothers and sisters to help me along the way. Friends that truly have become family, and you know who you are. But for my blood sisters and my brother, I wouldn't change them for anything.

Growing up as a kid, I always wanted to do well in school. After graduating high school, one of my desires was to go to Greensboro, North Carolina to live with my Uncle John and his wife, Aunt Minnie; who had no children as I recall. He was always nice to my mom who was his sister and my family. We loved visiting and staying with them at their home, and he always offered for me to come and stay. It was a little different than city living.

What Did You Say I Could Be?

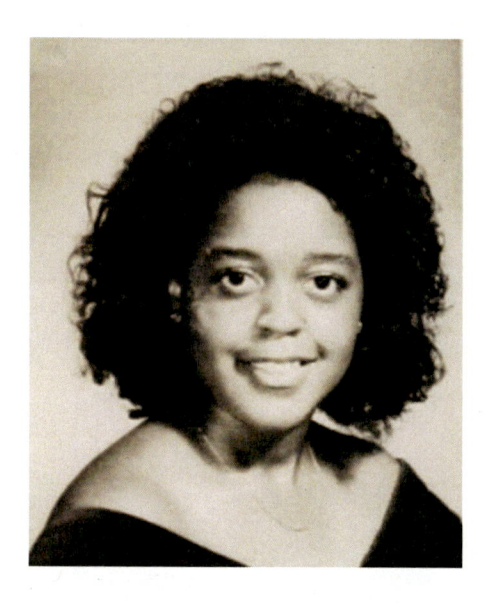

I also remember playing in my neighborhood, singing on the choir at school and church, and traveling to my grandparents' Marie Jones, my dad's mother, and Gela and Letchard Richardson my mom's parents' home every summer in South Boston, Virginia to be with my girl cousins. There were eight of us at any given time, or nine of us staying together for weeks all at the same time. Hey, I know now what free labor is all about. Even though I played most of the time. I remember we ate well because my grandparents had a farm with all sorts of animals, a vegetable garden, and fruit trees. Talk about plant based. I miss that. What I wouldn't give for that now. We played church regularly and made up all sorts of games. My cousins came from Virginia, New Jersey, and me from Maryland. It was always an exciting, fun, and eventful time.

Life was pretty carefree being the youngest of the family. I always had others looking out for me; my parents, sisters, brother, relatives, and friends etc.. We traveled a lot with my dad being a minister to see family and going to many other churches over the years. We also had fun trips to amusement parks, state fairs, and to see plays as well. I loved to sing when I was younger. At school as I mentioned and in the church choir of my sister's new church. I led many songs and was also in a few singing groups. I was a part of various fashion shows in middle and high school. Winning numerous competitions in fashion shows and becoming the Homecoming Queen of my graduating class of 1981 in high school. I loved the performing arts, and attended Paul Laurence Dunbar High School in Baltimore, Maryland.

All my siblings did get along with each other. We grew up and attended our father's church. My siblings along with a few others who attended my father's church also went to Dunbar High School in Baltimore. I remember going there quite often before I became a student earlier on with my brother Donnal. He was part of the band, with Mr. Anderson and I enjoyed hanging out with him often in the band room, and at many events there. Most people thought I was already a student because of how often I would be there.

I also became a lover of decorating, and design as I stated. I always had creative ideas and enjoyed creating things with my hands, and sewing a little along with my mom. She enjoyed making hats and clothes; and she taught me how to sew as well. I loved roller skating, going to the movies, traveling, and also going to IHOP (International House of Pancakes) on Friday nights after church services. It was the only place that was open late, lol. We had choir anniversaries each year and these were always fun. We would prepare for the choir anniversaries rehearsal after rehearsal. We also would love to go out to a nice restaurant when the event was over.

My sister-in-law by marriage and choir director playwright Joyce Queen Esther Elizabeth Diggs. I had to say it. It was the longest name I ever heard since hearing of my grandmother's full maiden name (my maternal grandmother). Gela Oakley Evelyn Blanchie Carrie Francis Downey Richardson. What a mouthful! Joyce became my third sister by marriage. She would reserve a place for all of us to go for dinner. This was her contribution to us for all of our hard work and dedication for the choir anniversary event. We had a big dinner out together and celebrated afterward usually at Flagship or Hogates in Washington, DC. Sometimes it would be 20 to 30 of us. We had a blast. It was always a highlight each year. Again, I was always the youngest member of the group. However, I always had so many brothers and sisters to look up to, and watch out for Baby Zelda as my brother-in-law Clarence nicknamed me. I get so full and emotional when I hear the song, *The Church I Grew Up In* by Tasha Cobbs. STOP and go listen to this song! Did you feel it too! "Why I am the way I am... it's the church I grew up in."

One of my 9th grade dreams was to become an interior decorator. Even though at the time I really didn't understand truly what was required. I just recall always rearranging the furniture in our home. Especially during the summer months when I was out of school. My mother would come home from work to find things often rearranged. My bedroom, living room, dining room, sun porch etc..

I always loved creating things. So of course, interior designing was a natural interest and profession for me. I went back to school and attended college 20 years later after high school for interior design. It's never too late. I was told God's delay is not his denial. Remember that! Although I believed I would be a good marketer and event planner as well. I feel I have always been someone who tries to solve issues and come up with ideas and creative ways to do many things. My sister Belinda and I would call it our "bed and breakfast experience" because from a discussion of creating a quaint bed and breakfast idea, we went out on a huge tangent and before we knew it, we had designed a full blown hotel; and so now we call it "our bed and breakfast inside joke." I've actually had several jobs, but my top job is being a decorator's assistant in Atlanta, Georgia and in Columbia, Maryland. I also worked as a front desk receptionist for a decorating furniture company. I was always working around and assisting designers and clients at the Ethan Allen design center in Maryland. I loved that job!

Hopes, Dreams and Fears, Oh My!

Also, I have said this in the past, one of my dreams was to have a good marriage relationship and to be an example to others. When I was a child/teen I would always say "I would make someone a good wife." "Two times the charm." During my young adult years, my greatest fear was maybe getting in trouble at church with my dad being the pastor or getting a bad grade in school. I was fearful when becoming pregnant and being a single parent. Yes, these were some of my own hope, dreams, and fears.

There were times when my friends and I would be together. I would sneak and go to places mainly dances or a party here and there. Probably some activities I did not have permission to go to. Most of the time my brother made sure I was straight by dropping me off and picking me up. I told you he was my ride or die. Well, mainly my ride.

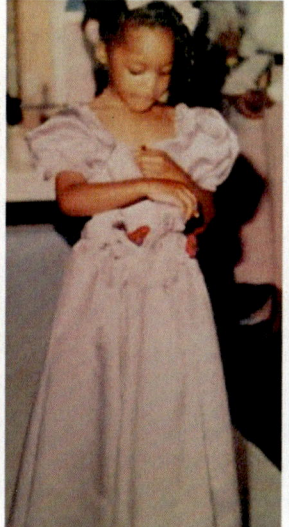

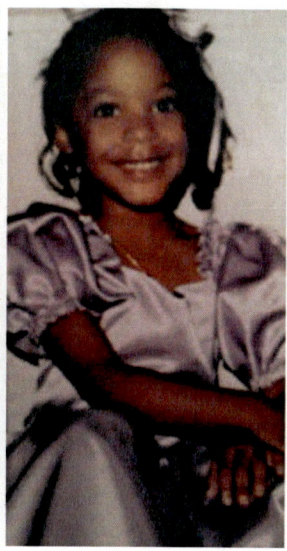

Love Connections

    Remember that show *Love Connection*? Well, let's just say, this was the beginning of mine. I dated Fred Thompson prior to me leaving to go to Richmond, Virginia. When I became bored being in Richmond, I decided to return back to Baltimore. Our initial connection actually came out of attending what I considered my second church with my sister Diana after she became married. I used to attend and sing on the choir there. I recall my sister's sister in law (Joyce) and choir director used to bargain for me to come and lead songs for her choir at different churches and on special occasions. Each Labor Day weekend there was a tradition where my dad would preach, we would sing, and participate in an annual play in Newark, New Jersey and Waterbury, Connecticut. Hey, I never knew I was a bargaining chip. Oh well as I was saying, Fred's family was also a musical singing family. We were both young and I guess that puppy love started to grow. You know, the stage when as a teenager you think you know everything. The phase that all teenagers have a tendency to go through. We both became young parents without truly understanding the magnitude and responsibility that comes along with being a parent. Bringing another life into the world can be beautiful but it is no easy task. However, just being who I am, I was determined, and I knew I wanted our daughter Crystal to have the best life that I could give her. I didn't want to become another statistic.

I remember finding out that I was pregnant at 18 years old, and would soon be a single teenage mom. You may be seeing a pattern here with me. It's never just one event this time it's two. First let's go back to when I became pregnant. Believe it or not I'm still trying to wrap my head around this because of where I now have found myself ending up in this life's journey. I graduated high school not knowing exactly which direction I was going to go. Okay, somebody still has some explaining to do. I can't even recall my conversation with my guidance counselors at the end of high school, and what my plans were going to be for the future. However, being the youngest of the four of all my siblings. Following in the footsteps of most of my church friends and associates who went to Dunbar high school. By the way, we had the best undefeated basketball team around and our football team was not too shabby either. Also, I was the homecoming queen class of '81 thank you, thank you, thank you very much (in my Elvis voice). A very proud moment for me at an early age. Looking back, having fun but not really paying enough attention to the future as I probably should have done. I found myself in this place.

Seeing my dad cry when finding out I was pregnant; I will never forget. Not to mention having to tell both my parents of this occurrence. Telling my mom that I was pregnant was heartbreaking as well. During the time of my pregnancy, I worked away from my parents' home at a friend of my mom's senior adult living facility; as a nanny for her two grandchildren. I felt ashamed and guilty because I had been taught to have a baby outside of marriage was wrong and would be hard. However, I had support in many different forms.

My oldest sister Belinda was the only one to complete and graduate from college and that was all on her own. My other sister Diana attempted to follow in her footsteps but became gainfully employed instead. My brother Donnal after high school was not engaged either in higher education. He had a brief encounter in the military but ended up in the workforce as well. My parents were not college educated, so that was not an option in the forefront of all our minds. With all that being said and in front of me, I knew what I had an interest in doing but I really did not know how to pursue it. Interior designing that is. Before I get ahead of myself. I graduated from high school, and I had an offer from my very close cousin Elizabeth, and my aunt to come and stay in Richmond, Virginia. This invitation would give me some time to figure out what I wanted to do with my life.

Looking back now it really is a tall order for any 17 or 18 year old to really have a clue on what direction you would like for your life to go. Honestly, what in the world do we truly know then. Oh well, I guess that is why life is called trial and error! Or "Whatever doesn't kill you makes you stronger." I have my thoughts on all of the clichés we grew up with. I may speak to that later on.

Okay Zee, stick to the story. I went to Richmond excited and scared but loved it at first. Then home sickness set in and six months later I returned to Baltimore. She's back! I reconnected with my old beau and became pregnant. I guess I was a little too homesick. Right then, in a moment my life would change forever. Stress I don't think is the word. There were so many emotions, feelings, thoughts, and "what ifs" going through my head. You remember, as I said I was a teenager. Oh yes, and a preachers kid. I recall the disappointment on my mom's face. If it weren't for my faith and my belief in God, I would not have made it.

After I became pregnant. Oh boy! I must say a lot of my conviction came when I attended church services. I felt really horrible. I felt like I let my family down, mainly my parents. I let myself down, but mostly I was afraid that I let God down. It left an impression on my heart and in my mind that I will never forget. It broke my heart even more. As I stated before, my mom was disappointed but really very supportive. Both of my sisters and my brother were in my corner. I always felt love and support from them all. So forever grateful for my cousin, Helen Dunn, who took me in her home once I was back in Virginia. She helped guide me and showed me the way to understand that life wasn't over for me. I just needed to refocus.

When I became pregnant, and knew my life was really about to change, I asked what I felt was a stupid question. "Why Me?" Already knowing the answer. Because silly you should not have been engaged in what you knew the outcome and consequences could be. All I could do is ask God to help me through it and have mercy on me.

The negative for me that I can remember was a scare tactic. My father threatened me by saying… that if by chance I got pregnant; my house would become like a prison. Well that didn't work. Not realizing and knowing how to have a conversation about life. How our bodies are changing. The do's and don'ts and the why's. All the actions you take have consequences and results for life. Honest communication could have been much better on the part of my parents and me. Along with better listening, believing, and understanding on my part.

Even though I'm sure it took my parents a little time to come around. My siblings were always very supportive of me during this time. With the way the world has become today it is important to not lose your principles and the foundation of what the Word of God says, and what we are taught to believe. Having a little more positive understanding instead of the negative is needed.

I felt sad at times that my life somehow had slipped away and that being pregnant would change everything. The fear of the unknown was very scary. Once I realized that I had a forgiving God and forgiving parents and that this was not the end of the world; and my life was not over, then I started to breathe again. I started making plans and what seemed to be better decisions for my life. Not only for me, but as a new young mother, and for my little heartbeat, Crystal Danyelle. I recommitted my life to Christ.

Trusting God and Yourself – The True Connection

    I've had many learning experiences. I feel my only regret is in the big grand scheme of things we call life; we sometimes have to learn through experiences before we can truly know what there is to know. What there is to know to make it through this life. We seem to not reach that until we are much older. I have truly learned of course, to trust God, but also to trust myself. God created us all in different ways, with different paths and experiences; in life mine differs from yours and yours from mine. That's why I understand the scripture that says, *"Judge not, lest ye be judged." Do not judge or you will be judged. For in the same way you judge others, you will be judged and with the measure you use, it will be measured to you.* **Matthew 7:1-2**. Having someone judge you, especially in a negative way, never feels good. It's often said. Everyone has a story. Also, as the saying goes. "You may see my glory, but you don't know my story." I've also learned that my wholehearted attempt in life is to love unconditionally. Yes, I do have feelings and a few exceptions in general. One being just having overall respect for each other. It goes a long way. No one is ever perfect. When I couldn't see my way, He made a way. All right now. I think this is the point here for a "Thank You Jesus." Hallelujah. Praise break is due, OK, I'm back. When you get older the sayings of your youth tend to mean so much more to you. I believe because you have grown and have a deeper understanding and meaning. Now, I can relate to the sayings of the older members and my parents growing up in church. When they would say, *"When I think of the goodness of Jesus, and all He has done for me. My soul cries out, Hallelujah, thank God for saving me."* Not only my soul from so much but mainly saving me from my wrong way of thinking, and saving me from myself.

The healing process happened over time, I guess you can say. During my pregnancy, I know I felt scared back then. Spiritually as well as physically. Spiritually, because I felt I let God down. Physically because being a pregnant teen and the outward presence that I could not hide. I guess simultaneously both were taking place which had me conflicted about who I was created to be. But God!

Being born into and brought up in a Christian home and being faith based; I was always surrounded by positive messages and testimonies. I would constantly hear positive encouraging sayings from people. It seemed no matter what anyone around me was facing or going through, they tried to have a good outlook on their situations. Always proclaiming at the end, that God is good! So, when negative thoughts or situations came my way, being in the presence of God and the constant atmosphere of church would see me through. My father would be preaching and proclaiming faith through his sermons and my mother would play the piano and sing encouraging songs. I always had what I considered a strong positive faith mindset. However, there was also one other memorable bad experience I went through. It was my divorce. Of course, entering into a marriage relationship. You don't foresee separation or divorce in the beginning. At least I didn't. Although, I must say the process itself was not as bad as some. But the pain in this disconnection was not a pleasant experience either. Your hopes and dreams of building a life with someone that turns out to not be the case is upsetting. You feel as though you have wasted so much of your time or just failed in life. However, everything happens for a reason. God said, he would restore what was taken away from you in many cases **(Joel 2:25).** I know He ultimately did it for me! I know if He did it for me, He can do it for you!

It's a scripture in the Bible that I always stand on. *"All things work together for good to them that love the Lord, and called according to his purpose"*

(Romans 8:28). So all means all. The good, the bad, the ugly, the triumphs, the losses, the victories. They all have and still are working for my ultimate good. Why? Because I love the Lord with all my heart, soul, and mind. And I know I'm called for a specific purpose for Him. So I have learned over time to take the good and the bad. Because into each life, some rain truly must fall. You just have to have the right umbrella covering. The sunshine will eventually shine again with a few rainbows from time to time. How beautiful are the rainbows. You have to get through it! Life is tough at times. Some come into your life for a reason, a season, or a lifetime. We all have to adjust. We all lose loved ones as well. You know your parents will one day leave you. I wasn't prepared for my only brother Donnal, who I loved so much, to leave me at 50 years old. That was one bad experience you never see coming. No matter what happens in life, you often try to prepare yourself for any type of loss. I am forever grateful for God being there to see me through.

I often try to do and accomplish things without expecting anything special in return. I am long past that, just hopefully to bring a more positive perspective to others. Possibly the way we view things and what our existence truly means. I also have cosigned a saying. Most say that life is too short, but I heard one of my indirect mentor's, Shedrick White, say. "It's not that life is too short; we just take too long to start living it." My challenge to you is that "You choose to live life, and don't let life live you."

I would like to pass it on to others. To be intentional about your life. I was taught and often heard and quoted. *"Train up a child in the way that he or she should go, and when they get old, they will not depart from it"* **(Proverbs 22:6)**. Try to have a game plan for life as early as you can. Yes, we know everyone is going to grow up to be their own authentic selves. We know there is no ultimate blueprint when we enter this world. As I probably stated before. Other than for me being fortunate enough to have the Bible to learn, lead and guide, which became my blueprint. However, for some that may not have been that way from the start. I heard a successful NBA dad who has three sons playing in the league state once that *"We should not necessarily push our children; instead, we should lead them because when we push them it may cause them to resist."* So I feel it's better to be the example as best you can and lead them. We were often told. As children, *"Don't do as I do. Do as I say do."* Or *"Children were meant to be seen and not heard."* Well, it's a different generation and a different day and time. And we must be the example. The scripture says, *"To be doers of the word and not just hearers only."* Also, *"Faith without works is dead."* (James 2:26).

I don't have many regrets. But I do have a few do overs. If I could have done this or that a little differently are sometimes in my thoughts. My husband Adrian loves the book of proverbs. I do also. It is truly a book of wisdom, as it is called. The Bible itself is a good learning ground for life. I think once you read, research, and meditate on it regardless of any questions you may have there is an incident or similar occurrence stated in the Bible that relates to all situations. I believe it starts first with faith we all can believe and have faith in many things as we all do. Even though we may not have all the answers. I choose to rely on what I do know and have experienced and felt inwardly. There is an old song that says, *This Joy I Have The World Didn't Give It To Me And The World Can't Take It Away*. You have to experience it to truly believe it. It's a beautiful blueprint to live by. However, Proverbs is a wonderful starting point. If we can master that book, I truly believe the rest of the book and life itself would be a whole lot easier. A chapter a day will help you in every way.

A Fork in the Road – Me, Myself, and I

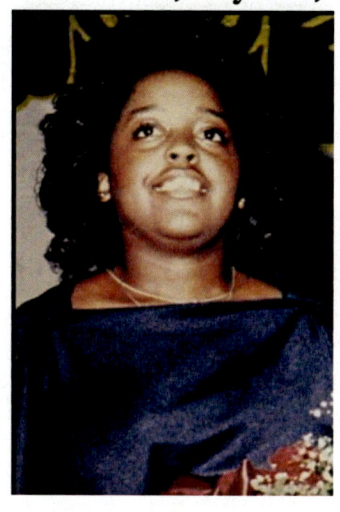

I went on to cosmetology school, graduated, and became certified as a cosmetologist. However, I always liked decorating, but cosmetology was my second choice and easier at the time to get into. I was always told I had beautiful hair and styled it very well. That prompted me to enter the hair industry, and pursue cosmetology as a career. However, more and more I started to realize who I was. What I had been taught along with who God really was in my life. No longer was it just about me, but now I had another life to be concerned about. Looking back, I really had to rely on God. Sometimes during challenging times. You do really realize how much you need His guidance. Today, years later, the song, *"Never would have made it,"* also rings true for me. It was truly by his grace, mercy, and guidance that I made it not only through the good times, but most importantly not giving up during the rough times. All because of His grace and truly His mercy.

Working to Find My Way

My first real paying job was a sales associate at the Gap clothing store at Reisterstown Road Plaza in Baltimore Maryland. I was about 17 years old in high school. One of my most challenging jobs I had was being a kindergarten assistant teacher. Although I can say it was rewarding at times and I adored the children; I have always stated that teaching children was not my purpose or calling. I did have a couple of other jobs that I loved. As I mentioned before, I was a designer assistant in both Atlanta and in Maryland. I also worked for the Ethan Allen furniture design center. While working at several hair salons over the years, and also at the design center, I truly enjoyed all of those experiences. Especially the design center until there were certain administrative responsibilities that were placed upon me which was not mentioned prior to me acquiring the position. I found that the task, which was a major one, was not part of my job description nor came with a higher increase in pay. It was someone else's responsibility that no longer wanted to do it and that duty was placed upon me, and it became very stressful. I believe there is good stress that can help you grow and bad stress that can stunt your creativity along with productivity and ultimately your growth. Some would say bad stress makes you stronger. I believe yes and no. Challenging stress occasionally. However, bad stress day in and day out, I believe can kill your spirit and your soul. Stress may also affect your body and your mind and sometimes your overall health. We are afraid to sometimes admit it until it's too late. Your creativity can be stifled and no longer effective.

Hair has always been my second choice, and decorating had always been my first choice. I was becoming a former hairstylist and cosmetologist for over 30 years. At the time I felt it was easier getting into doing hair than decorating. So I pursued doing hair which became my livelihood but as fate would have it I went back to school for interior design 20 years later after high school. This was the very same school I read about in a magazine years ago. When I read the article I became interested in attending this school. I found the same college in Atlanta. Who knew, but God? I also worked for a bridal stationary company briefly that sold t-shirts, invitations, and bridal accessories. I really enjoyed it. It was one of my more secluded peaceful and quiet jobs. I have found while growing up that I have always loved the creative process. Creating my own hairstyles, admiring architectural buildings, paintings, pictures, colors, making things etc.. I have always been fascinated by how things start and what it ultimately becomes in the end. As I stated before, many summers and times throughout the year, my parents would come home to see the furniture and other aesthetics within the home rearranged. It's like we had a new house. Well, in my mind.

Entrepreneurship and Being An Author

My former and last occupations were a hairstylist, interior design assistant, travel agent, and entrepreneur for my husband and myself (THE A2ZExperience brand). My status now is a stay-at-home wife which I am very blessed to be able to do, due to health reasons. Did you say blessed? I do feel it has been a blessing in disguise. It changed me. I am now a writer (who knew) along with helping to build a brand and an entrepreneurship future for my husband and myself. I am also able to be engaged in more family activities without constraint. Now, I am traveling with my husband more frequently for his job and business; while visiting my daughters and sisters in other states. I am blessed to say that do to my network marketing groups, Mad Team (Valencia Pamphile, Art Lee, and my brother by way of my brother, Brandon Missouri) and Plannet Marketing (Mr. Donald Bradley, Joy Dawkins), I am forever grateful to these groups, along with my travels with my parents, and my husband Adrian; I have traveled to over 40 plus states and a few international countries.

Being a stay-at-home wife has allowed me to become the woman I feel I was destined to be. To take care of my husband, relate more, and be involved with my family and friends. I also seek God more quietly and freely. To focus in on Him in such a more real intentional way is hard to describe sometimes. But to focus in on Him without distractions, has been enriching, beautiful and a rewarding experience. So, yes, do I think I would change my past occupation. Well, I believe it changed automatically for me in the most wonderful way. Entrepreneurship has always been in my blood for quite some time. The saying goes " *It's not always how you start but how you inish.*" Being able to write a book which is something that I never imagined for me, and it shows, "*That the latter days shall be greater than our former days*" is what my inspirational guidebook tells me. I'm just glad for all my past work experiences. However, I believe they made me stronger as of today in many ways.

Growing up Mentally – What You See Is What You...

My attitude from childhood to adulthood, I must say, hasn't changed a whole lot. Other than my attitude has evolved and has grown bigger. I don't know. I have people in my life, my sisters, some long standing friends. Even my now husband that I had not seen in 30 plus years will say that you are still the same. He calls me his little Baby Zelda as my brother-in-law who is now deceased used to call me in my early years. My husband also calls me Zpooh, and this is similar to Zella pooh a name my grandmother Gee Gee used to call me. I've always been mostly positive... an ambitious, curious, go getter, big eyed little girl that loved to do things her own way. I loved to go places, explore, and create things. I enjoyed cheering and seeing others succeed as well. I was a giver of ideas back then to my friends and even now. I try to share what I have been given. Not always monetarily, but in knowledge, opportunities, resources, and ideas. I always talk and can give advice. Oh yeah, give advice I know sometimes I can find myself needing to take my own. Sometimes we all often do.

I really believe when I look back over my life and my development stage; I have what I heard someone say, "May I have a few do-overs, please?" Ultimately, I am proud of who I have grown up to be. Wow!

I don't think I have ever said that out loud. Wow! (tears are definitely flowing). I felt that sometimes you feel like you were different for so long, then you grow to realize that you were okay after all. You are who God created you to be. One thing that I love about myself is that I try very hard not to be judgmental. I try not to stay long in my own pity party. I love just as my mother, to treat everyone with the same respect and kindness. I have always believed and continue to treat and respect the janitor, housekeeper, and maid; as I would a millionaire, CEO or even a billionaire and I've had the pleasure of sitting, communicating, and enjoying each of their company. I truly understand the statement, Black Lives Matter. Your life matters. My life matters. All lives matter. Respect has to be there on all levels, and in all cases. Treating others as you would want to be treated. My husband and I heard a term once that we have now adopted. *"If you do good you do well and if you do well you do good."* In essence, be kind and do the right thing, and it will come back to you.

I believe most people would say that I have a positive outlook on mostly everything. I always try to see the bright side of things or always have a solution in mind. Possibly my giving nature in these latter years. My earlier years maybe not too much. Only because I attribute that to my dad. It's not that he wasn't a giving person. He was an only child, so he had a challenge with sharing. Okay, I think I said that the best way right? Being an only child, he taught me being the baby, I guess how everything seemed to be mine. I can remember him buying me things and would emphasize how this is just for me. You can't tell the youngest of the family that too often.

Also, my family and friends may say my worst attribute may be my stubbornness. Of course I may think mostly in a good way but also in a challenging way. Being the baby and the youngest of the family, I have my thoughts and ways of how I see things being done. I guess to sum it up; once my brother Donnal had a conversation with my oldest sister Belinda. He told her in any given situation he and she would be talking about it, and my sister Diana would be praying about it; and I would have already done it. What can you say about those babies of the family? You have got to love them!

CHAPTER 2

EXPLORING BEAUTIFUL RELATIONSHIPS LOVE AND MARRIAGE AND EVERYTHING IN BETWEEN

―――◆―――

I met my first husband, Isaac Hampton in Washington, DC at a Christian conference through my very close cousin Elizabeth who went to high school with him in Richmond, Virginia. I met him again at the price club, now known as Costco, today, where he worked at the time. Since being a single mom for the past three years and trying to maneuver single parenting, it was refreshing to meet someone new and different. I felt pretty secure and hopeful.

Now being brought up in the church all my life, the one thing I will never forget my cousin's saying to me before I met him. Is that, and I quote, *"He Is Really Saved."* For those who don't know, once you make a decision to give your life to Christ, you stop doing or you are supposed to stop doing the things that separate you from God and start doing the things to bring you closer to Him. Your life is changed, and you do actually try to live by the standard of *"What Would Jesus Do?"* Then allow Him to help guide your life. Well let's just say he was a man my cousin knew. I had to be ready and serious about my faith and belief. Because as she said, *"He was Really Saved."* Since seventeen years of age, he was serious. He was not playing around.

Hey, now that I think about it. What did she mean? I was serious, with my single mom self. Okay, I must say she was right. We did eventually meet, connected, and dated. We got married and had a beautiful daughter we named Erica. He was accepting of my daughter Crystal at the time being so young. He treated and connected with her just like she was his very own. He went on to step in and be the father figure to her that she needed. I will be forever grateful for that. He was a praying man and serious about God. In my first marriage, in the beginning we were building a life together; spiritually, financially, and with family and friends. Connections were being made. We had some fun times, happy times, and growing and learning times.

Honestly, I was very truthful with him. We spoke each other's spiritual language, I guess. Both being brought up in the church, he says. It was the sound of my voice. He thought I was an evangelist. I don't know if I would use that word! WHOA! Only because it was a bit challenging at the start because remember I had a child. His parents really didn't smile upon that at times. I drew him with my honesty and humor. I always loved to laugh. It's a family thing. My entire family enjoyed laughter. My mom, dad, sisters, and brother. We all had it! We all loved engaging with people, and he loved to laugh as well. Oh yeah, we both could sing also, and we did sing together publicly at churches and events.

He proposed to me on Valentine's Day in 1987, and I said, *"Yes"* even though his parents weren't too happy about him having a ready-made family. I recall more so his dad having reservations. My mother-in-law, Roselee Hampton and I grew to be like mother and daughter until this day. I will forever be grateful for her love and support towards me and my daughter, Crystal. My father-in-law eventually came around once he saw I had good intentions and meant his son no harm only good. Rest in Heaven (R.I.H.) Dad Hampton.

Our wedding was at a beautiful church in Richmond, Virginia with 250 plus guests in attendance. My uncle Robert L Tapper and my father Morris R Lane both officiated. We had a host of bridesmaids, groomsmen, my ring bearer, and with my little four year old daughter, Crystal being our flower girl. So cute. I was excited at the time as any girl would be on a day you may have dreamed about growing up. This was my moment, and I was scared and unaware of what the future had in store for us. I was ready to take that leap of faith and I was really only hoping and praying for the best. I do have a word of advice. It's OK to be excited about the wedding but be just as or even more excited and intentional about the marriage in the future.

As you get older, you realize marriage can be beautiful. However, marriage is work. You get out of it what you both ultimately put into it most of the time; along with reaping some blessings and rewards along the way. It is important to keep God at the center of all that you do. I now know that it's easier said than done. My hopes were that my marriage would grow and become an example for others. That has always been my heart's desire. I truly wanted that, and I wanted to be married. As I stated earlier, I can remember saying, for whatever reason, as a teenager, I would make someone a good wife. I always felt that deep down inside of me.

We were together for 23 years. One thing I do recall is that we spent most of our time in church and a lot of time on helping to build a ministry, but perhaps not enough time building us. Toward the end of our marriage things for me started to unravel. My grandmother who helped raise me died, then the love of my life, my mom unexpectedly followed a year later. The decision I finally made inside is partially due to something the doctor stated to my sister. While my mother lay in a coma after having a stroke. Relying on a respirator to keep her breathing alive, she formulated a blood aneurysm in the lower back portion of her head. They felt it was too risky to operate at her age being 80 years old. The doctor stated that my mother had no signs of fighting to live because she was dying of a broken heart. Broken Heart! I recall hearing that term before only in theory. But to hear someone say this in the case of someone I loved so dear, changed something inside of me.

Just a thought of someone not wanting to fight to live because their heart has been broken. I don't know until this day all my mother may have went through, but I do know that I did not want to go out like that. I recall telling my siblings in the waiting room after seeing my mother lying there helpless. I spoke to each of them pointing my finger at them in the waiting room of the hospital at the same time. I let them know that *"I would not go out like that,"* those were my exact words.

Even before that moment I found myself stressing, very unhappy and realizing that God had more life for me to live than what I was experiencing. I realize there could be a strong opinion about going versus staying. To divorce or not to divorce that is the question? So it is written, *"Hope deferred makes the heart sick."* All I can say for me is that my heart and life had become unhealthy in more ways than one. Since making that decision in my life, my purpose became more clear and fulfilled. In spite of all the challenges, I'm happier than I ever thought I could be. Or may I say dreamed of being. In the book, I read **Ephesians 3:20** *God says that "Now unto Him that is able to do exceedingly abundantly above all that we ask or think," according to the power that worketh in us."* Even though it was a difficult decision, I have my exceedingly, abundantly, …in the form of Adrian Johnson.

Beginning of the End – The Wonder Years

My marriage began to crumble because I felt as though we did grow apart. I really don't want to sound cliché or place the blame on any one thing. Nor did we seek professional counseling. How-ever, we both were simply not on the same page. I don't think adequate support and counseling was made available to us back then through our church affiliation at the time. Nor did we seek counsel. As I began to grow. I realized it felt as if God had so much more for me in life. I just didn't see it going in that direction. In sum, over time we had become strangers.

Based upon what I know about relationships, and marriages (which is one of the most sacred unions) it should not be a tug of war and battle for the ages. OK, I may be going a little overboard. However, I do believe professional counseling should be an option. It's a very necessary tool that I feel could help in any relationship case. Life is hard. We could argue our points all day. But it can also be beautiful. However, if we don't come together and sometimes agree to disagree, then you will never have a peaceful, happy, and productive life or marriage. I'm just saying.

There are so many scriptures I could use to try and justify my decision. However, I choose not to do this. I do believe God is the author and finisher of our faith. It came down to what I was ultimately believing for my life as I continue to discover God's plan for my future. I do believe now more so than ever that the wedding vowels you say and commitment you make to each other when becoming married; is not just a cute saying to repeat during the ceremony. I believe we have been conditioned to repeat words, but we must really believe and act on them in order to have a successful marriage. Writing a heartfelt expression of your own words and feelings to each other may be more beneficial. The commitment to each other may go further and help to get you through the future and hard times. Not just because you repeated what was required. I came to truly find that I wanted more out of life than what was being given. Selfish as it may seem, but necessary for the growth, development, and purpose God has deemed for my life.

My Happily Ever After: Adrian S. Johnson

"The Darker the Berry the Sweeter the Juice"
Watch Out Now!

I met Adrian in the Spring of 1979 at Morgan State University. My high school, Paul Laurence Dunbar was holding a dance at the University. Well, we will return back to this a little later on. Zelda, Zelda, Zelda what were you thinking? Let's just say, *"It was the best of times, and it was the worst of times."* The decisions we make. I feel writing about my now husband, Adrian, could possibly take up most of the chapters in the book. Before Fred or Isaac came into the picture, Adrian was the original gangster (OG). One thing led to another and being young and not sure of myself, it was over before it really got started. I ended up breaking it off with him and moving on. Even though I made a change to be with my oldest daughter's father, things just were not meant to be. The signs were all there, so I choose to move back to Richmond, Virginia as I stated. There is where I met my first husband Isaac as noted above.

One of my regrets or "Do overs as I call them." Is being young, and inexperience in life and relationships. Breaking it off with Adrian was difficult and the pain and hurt that it caused both of us at the time was difficult. Let's just say the breakup was real hard on both of us.

Even though we were young, we know now that it's all a part of life. It's never easy or feels good to end relationships. The truth is that it affects all involved. Whether good or bad. Whether we want to admit it or not.

Our first relationship ended as several of others do, because I allowed someone else to come in between us. Feeling the grass was greener on the other side. Which somehow always takes you back to the "what ifs." Let me not get ahead of myself. When I met Adrian, he will tell you that I was his first real girlfriend. He was the best boyfriend I ever had. We had a great time together. He had his own car, his own job, his own money. Need I go on. Very free and independent. No major hassles with us at all.

I was young and dumb right? Ok, let's just call it what it was. Young, frisky, flirty, and confused. Ok, I said it. He was a few years older than me. A little more focused on life and going in the direction of what he possibly wanted. I was more free and flowing. Always saying at an early age, I would make someone a good wife. I guess I just didn't want to follow the plan at 15 ½. Well, I rounded my age up to 16 years old. Only because I felt I was closest to it and tried to be more mature. Alright grown. I didn't realize I was dealing with a numbers guy. He quickly figured my true age out. The one thing I will really always cherish. Adrian was an upstanding guy that I could count on then and until this day. So much so that after our breakup, almost two years later; I had the audacity to call him up and ask him to my senior prom. To be honest he was the only guy that I wanted to take me to my prom. It was fun and beautiful. However, mixed feelings on my part prevented me once again from reigniting our relationship. Second time I had the chance and opportunity. "Zelda, Zelda, Zelda! What were you really thinking?" I did find out from him; all he was doing was accommodating a friend. We attended the prom. His first ever, my second. We parted ways once again.

Fast forward after some time went by between Adrian and myself, for me the dreaded phone conversation I had to make for some odd reason to him. Unfortunately, I had to inform him that I was pregnant with someone else's child. What a blow! Now to realize that was part of his dream for the future. Lesson learned. He said he hung up the phone and said, "Well I guess that is the end of that." (He's still saying today we would have had five children). The decisions we make can affect our future and others so much. He always says to me, I've had a pretty good childhood and overall good life. In most cases I have been blessed to have many positive experiences. Well believe it or not the story during our early years didn't end there. Possibly a third chance, with my hand on my head.

Now living back in Virginia, I was visiting Baltimore with my two year old daughter. Things weren't happening in no way with her biological father. I reached out to my friend once again. We ended up talking. For whatever reason I wanted him to at least meet my daughter. Not only did he meet us he drove us back to Richmond, Virginia. That's just the kind of guy he was (then and now). We spoke probably a few times after that encounter. Then time stepped in, and we never spoke until 30 years later. However, those "What if's" I'm sure stays with most of us throughout our lives. As you can already see, I feel talking about my husband Adrian could possibly take up chapters, and I could write an entire book called "Then & Now" The Adrian Johnson (AACUC) inside joke. Thanks Opal!

After going through life's ups and downs, we somehow ended up here. After my divorce, I found myself back in my home city of Baltimore, Maryland. How the heck did I get here? I would always say about Baltimore, "I love my city, and my family and friends that are still there, but I'm not going back there." I had several other places I was looking to explore, Dallas, Houston, Chicago, and even Kuwait. I have friends in all those areas who I was connected to, and I was extended an invite if I ever wanted it. However, I know today that God had another plan and like a chess board, He had all the players in the game for a queen that desperately needed to get back to where God wanted her to be.

Using the very thing I have always loved. Interior designing. I worked for my now dear friend Michele Ellis (at the time) as a design assistant when I lived in Atlanta. She knew I was looking for a change after my divorce and she contacted her friend Venetia Boyd another interior designer in Columbia, Maryland. Venetia became another dear friend, and she was also the photographer for our wedding in Atlanta, I might add. She was in need of another assistant. My sister Diana agreed to let me stay with her in Baltimore until I got myself established there. Time moved on and the swap was made from Atlanta to Maryland. I never would have thought this would happen. Well, I moved and reached out to some old friends and acquaintances. Adrian was who I wasn't quite sure I would recognize at first because it had been over thirty years. After somewhat coming to the conclusion with my sister. What do you know? It was him, right there on Facebook. I do recall asking my brother out of curiosity some years ago had he ever ran into him in Baltimore over the years. He said he had not. According to how he responded, AJ and I running joke is, he really wasn't trying to. He didn't want to start no trouble as my brother-in-law Dominic would say.

Well after reaching out to him on Facebook through a message and friend request. It took him a few days to respond and confirm. I thought it may be due to utter surprise and a state of shock. I was partially right. The other reason I later found out was that he was not sure if he wanted to confirm or ignore. Say What? However, I guess I really couldn't blame him. After all these years. Who Knew? Thankful for me and I believe I can speak for him also. That's one confirmation that we both have never regretted.

We exchanged numbers and talked. The one question after our second phone call Adrian asked and wanted to know. What happened and why did we break up? Yes, we were there already. I felt like it was a question he needed an answer to all his life. My heart racing, my past life flashing through my head like a movie on a screen. Then thinking about the question once again. The only answer that came to mind was an honest one. I was just too young at the time and made a not so wise decision. He told me later he was waiting to see if I would give him some lame answer. My answer turned out to be satisfying enough for him and one he said he couldn't argue with. We both were young. We had to leave it at that.

We decided to meet and catch up on old and current times. I drove down to pick him up from work. He left his car in the garage. We both could not believe it was us together again. He was a bit shocked because of me driving and picking him up. The last time we were together, I did not even have my driver's license. Our first encounter we held hands across the dinner table almost like we were picking up where we left off. After not seeing each other for so long. Laying eyes on each other once again and acknowledging the unspoken need for each other. We really couldn't believe it, but we could feel it. We drove down to Rusty Scuppers at the Baltimore Inner Harbor which is one of my favorite places to dine. I recall the waitress admiring us and asking, "How long had we been together"? We both smiled and said the first time in over 30 years. I felt like that sixteen year old girl again, OK, 15 and a half, I told him I was rounding up.

I am a witness that God gave me my desires and more! When you tap into God's vision for you and His will you won't go wrong. Remember, I said you also have to trust yourself and the instinct God placed inside of you. As we held hands, we acknowledged a deficit inside both of us, and being in need of each other. I had butterflies in my stomach. So excited to have laid eyes on him once again. We know now for a fact that saying for us rings true. *"If you truly love something set it free, and if it returns unto you it's yours and if it doesn't, then it never was."*

I am forever grateful that I returned. Let's come back to this. I told you I could write an entire book on us. I'm a firm believer in what Corinthians 13 states in the Bible….. *Love is patient, Love is kind….* Unfortunately, we have a tendency to override truth and principles. Proverbs along with Song Of Solomon have words to live by when it relates to wisdom and love.

Follow your true heart and your gut instinct. We do a lot of things in life just because and without rhyme or reason. Some things are subject to change. However, when you know you know. Not only trust God diligently but also you have to learn to trust yourself. Try to be an advocate of someone who loves love. When you do that I think it makes life a little easier and a little sweeter. Yes we know there is always the risk of getting hurt and disappointed. However, the bigger risk of never experiencing the love you so deserve also can be life altering. You have to give something if you say you love, and in return you shall receive. *God so loved the world that He gave His only begotten Son that whosoever ... (John 3:16).*

What God gave came to us, and set us free and remember it cost Him too. He was hurt giving his son to be sacrificed for us. We also may have to love, give, sacrifice but in the end the love that you feel is so unreal. Always look for that unreal love; that deep down in your gut feel love. But always know that the love is real and it's for you. Stop feeling unworthy. Take your time to study it, enjoy it, embrace it, feel it, cherish it, experience it! No one is ever perfect. Only God. We all have our imperfections. If we spend all of our time trying to change someone we will never get to the real true essence of a person. Yes, it's been said opposites attract. Well I believe not always. Like-minded people attract very well. I believe that's crucial. It makes life a little bit easier. You are not constantly butting heads on everything. I don't think that's how a healthy relationship should be. You may not understand some things because each of us may have been brought up with the same foundation and principles but still a different "how too." It's your choice if you're willing to compromise and move on in life and relationships. Also, remember sex is not love. It is only a physical act that can be in the confines of love. However, it is not necessarily love.

Love is so beautiful and can mean so many different things in so many different ways. Pray, explore, and choose what God has for you and ultimately what feels right for you. *"No good thing does he withhold from those who walk uprightly" (Psalms 84:11). Delight yourself in the Lord, and he will give you the desires of your heart (Psalms 37:1)*. Also, first find out who you are and what you truly want. It's okay. However long that may take is as long as it takes. There is a whole big world out here that God created. He created you, and it's all in what you desire. He created someone for you to live, love and enjoy it with. In the meantime, lock into you, family, friends, etc. to live the life that you imagined. I am a witness He gave me my desire and more!

Never Knew Love Like This Before

Never in a million years did I or we ever think that I would end up back here, in Baltimore and with my teenage sweetheart. You talk about a full circle moment. Can we say again, "Who Knew"? Being reunited with the love of my life is somewhat indescribable. Never did I ever. I said it before. Young and dumb. Can we just stop and play that game for a moment? Never Did I Ever…Only God Knew!

Reconnecting with my now husband Adrian feels like an "*Easy Like Sunday Morning*" moment. Ok, I'm now reaching back to the Commodores. If you know me you know I love music. I could probably write an entire chapter of our love story using songs. From me reaching out to him on Facebook to our first, second and third phone calls to our initial dinner encounter at Baltimore's Inner Harbor. Rusty Scuppers to be exact. We held hands across the table during dinner after not seeing each other in over thirty plus years. I think we were both in such disbelief to be looking at each other once again. Could this be truly real? As I stated before, we both acknowledged that we had a deficit, and were in need of each other. As time went on, we connected but it took a few moments for us to become reacquainted.

I recall one special occasion. It was Thanksgiving Eve, and the doorbell rang in Columbia, Maryland where I was working as a design assistant for my new designer Venetia. Her design center was laid out in the basement of her beautiful home. She comes downstairs with this beautiful bouquet of flowers and a beautiful orange ceramic pumpkin vase. My former coworker and now friend Michelle and I looked at each other. Venetia says, "For Zelda Lane." I was shocked and ecstatic. She says, "Now who gives flowers for Thanksgiving." Well, apparently the man of my dreams does. I said, "My Heavenly Father would do exceedingly and abundantly, didn't I?" Even though I knew he had some ties with others. (Hey, I just popped on the scene, remember? He had life going on, and so did I!) However, we knew we weren't going to let each other go once again. Life has a tendency to shape and mold you beyond what we can ever imagine. My heart believes we were molded from the beginning for each other. We constantly at times, even now continue to shake our heads in the realization of us being together. As fate would have it, well I really don't believe it was fate. I know it was God. We discovered we both were married the same month of the same year, and just on different days. We had no idea; I'm just saying.

Since our reconnecting and figuring it all out we have been *Inseparable*. Come on, Natalie Cole, I loved that song back then with him and now today it's probably one of my favorite theme songs for us. Along with *Amazing Love* by Luther Vandross, because Adrian knows I will follow him wherever he goes. *I Love Me Some Him* by Toni Braxton, K-Ci & JoJo, *All My Life* both songs danced to by my daughter Crystal at our wedding, and sung and covered by, *The Prayer*, Yolanda Adams & Donnie McClurkin sung by my daughter Erica, along with *Pieces of Me* by

Ledisi. Watch out now that will be in our next production. The wedding we had in Atlanta, Georgia among family and a few friends was priceless. Who would have ever imagined that we would be …Adrian says that God has a sense of humor. I say never say never.

    After all was said and done it was official and over. It was all systems go. We picked up where we left off. We dated, became engaged, and got married on January 1, 2017 on New Year's Day. It meant that those two teenagers who were still scared and somewhat fearful deep down inside; were finally having a chance together. We both knew this was a new beginning. A start of something special. We have gone through health challenges; and we love traveling with each other to different cities and states. We have enjoyed, football games, baseball games, and even an overnight and unexpected trip to Atlanta for the World Series. Adrian is such a laid back planner but also spontaneous and adventurous at times like me. We enjoy sharpening each other's iron. Good conversation is always present with us. We enjoy exploring life and we just enjoy being together. He's made me a better woman and even though he sent me his bio (inside joke)to catch me up on what he had been up to these thirty some plus years; to me, he's even a better man. We make each other better. Making up for lost time is an understatement. I realize we may never truly understand how all the twists and turns of life will ultimately play out. I do know we will be forever grateful for our second chance.

Having the opportunity of a second chance at life, a second chance at love with my anchor and my rock as he is now known. He has been the amazing highlight of my life. We've endured much in a shorter period of time, but we have gained something so rare and special that is lasting us a lifetime. To be able to live the rest of our life's journey together is a true blessing. Adrian says he truly feels it's a blessing and as I've said before, it feels like it's been a blessing in disguise. Beyond words at times. It's priceless to me. To experience a love so connected and so true, I believe is even necessary if you will. It was necessary for us to come back together. Not just for us but also for others and something greater than us. I know that may be a challenge for some to conceive or understand. I also know that there are others who may be feeling what I'm saying right now. Many have told us, and we agree that this is that meant to be kind of love. This is the kind of love that is meant to be cherished, recaptured, and to live out loud, now. The way it was designed to be before and into eternity.

A True Second Chance

There is a song by Phyllis Hyman called *Old Friend* recorded in 1986 that I love so much. She's one of my favorite artists. Even though this song wasn't recorded at the time we dated. This song was so meaningful to me when I reconnected with Adrian. The words are so fitting. I found my old friend, and my second chance. I don't have the rights to her music or the song. I will recommend you pause right here and go listen to the song. You'll be glad you did. Did you listen? Enough said.

Being reconnected back with my old friend has changed me in such a way. We have allowed each other to be the best versions of ourselves. I often say no one is perfect. But the love we share has penetrated my heart to a place that has overtaken and exceeded the desires of my heart. I am a firm believer that, *"Iron sharpens iron."* We sharpen each other, I often say. He just gets me, and I get him. We allow each other to be our authentic selves. His peaceful, straight forward, but quiet nature is so sexy to me. Okay, I forgot this is PG rated.

I've often heard it said, you can't find a good man or woman these days. Well I am so blessed to have my second chance. To have another chance at this thing called love and to walk this path of life unknown. Yes, we all have a past, and no one is perfect. But we all have a purpose and once you have the pleasure of finding yours. Don't hesitate! Walk it out with the love of your life as I am fortunate to do or even by yourself, do so. Time, Time ,Time. How much do we have? The enjoyment is in the knowing, exploring and the doing. My heart is overjoyed each day in the doing I get to experience with my Adrian.

Zelda D. Johnson

Chapter 3

Beauty Interrupted Surviving My Second Quarantine

———⚜———

"Oh, my goodness! What in the world?" This was my first response inwardly which I then began to verbally say out loud. I started to hear about this flu like virus starting to appear on the scene out of nowhere. Everyone was in disbelief. I had not quite thought much of it until later on, and I began to realize and come to grips with the fact that there was something major going on. Not only in other parts of the world but now right here in our country. I must say the thought ran through my mind when I began to hear often that several cruise ships were being affected. Some passengers and crew members were being held on board due to experiencing flu like symptoms and had contracted some type of virus.

This strange virus was causing ships to be unable to dock at some ports and not allowing passengers to leave the ships. Ships were sailing in from many places, but mainly passengers coming from China and that region had to stay on board and be quarantined for at least two weeks and sometimes even longer

You see this registered with me because I was a travel agent and had my own home-based travel business at the time. I found myself thinking even though no one is ever immune to hearing about negative occurrences within any industry; I was certainly concerned in regard to what I was hearing, despite not being fully involved with my business at that particular time due to my own personal health reasons. Oh yeah, we will come back to that a little later.

Honestly, when I began to listen more and more about the bans being placed domestically along with international travel, and people trying to get back to the United States from vacationing, and even business and military travel; I originally thought to myself, "here we go again." "Is it that serious?" After time began to pass and it began to become a widespread epidemic, I started noticing things becoming relatively serious not just on a weekly, but a daily basis. Prayer began to invade my heart with concern as to what is now known as coronavirus.

I never heard of or knew anything much about it, and it seemed others didn't either. Whenever I would have a conversation or hear others reference to all that was starting to take place, (mainly the many lives being lost), my heart truly became heavy. No one really knew exactly what it was, or how it was being contracted and spread throughout the country and in the world. However, we felt like we were dealing with a silent killer. I remember hearing across my TV screen who this daily assassin could and was ultimately affecting; seniors, the elderly anyone with underlying health conditions such as: hypertension, diabetes, a heart condition etc... What, Wait What? Did they say heart condition? This time it is more than, oh my goodness can we say, oh my God that is me! I am in that number. OK senior give or take a few, 56 at the time in my mind I am still borderline. Yeah, this just turned real personal.

Remember I said we would come back to my health issues? Well just to take you on a little personal journey, back in November of 2017, the day after Thanksgiving (Black Friday) to be exact, is when my life changed in the most dramatic way. It was just another relaxing holiday weekend for my honey and me. You see I have never been a big fan of getting out there in large crowds to shop during the holidays for some time now. However, I did plan and was waiting for an evening dinner planned with some of our very closest friends. Our friends included: The Walls and their mothers, the Bentleys (some of my husband's childhood friends), and us the Johnsons. It has become a little tradition that we continued through the years. We get together as couples; enjoying some good eating, laughter, and fellowship with one another. Waiting in expectation to ride into Maryland to meet my husband Adrian, who has his own little tradition of working the Friday after Thanksgiving. I drove down to an area to meet him where we continued to go to the restaurant in his car together. Seafood is one of our favorite foods and we love crab cakes that is since both of us are from Maryland. We all met and had a lovely evening of connecting and catching up since it was the start of the official holiday season. As my father would say after having such a delicious meal. "We have dined sufficiently." All of us gave one another hugs and said our goodbye wishes to each other. My husband and I left the restaurant and proceeded to retrieve my car for our ride home back to southern Pennsylvania.

We lived right across the Maryland Pennsylvania State line. However, not feeling any particular way during our celebratory evening, after getting my car; we proceeded to drive on 695 to 83 North. This is our usual journey home. Suddenly, a pain in the upper right side of my back began to ache. As I continued to drive, the pain became even more intense. My first thought was, *"Is this some sort of indigestion I'm having after having such a wonderful meal?"* And to know my usual practice half of my meal was taken home with me for later. Hey, wait a minute... what happened to my leftovers? Oh well, I was not feeling overindulgent in any way. However, I was starting to become more concerned, and feeling this intense pain that just would not let me go. I immediately pulled over on the highway only after an exit or so from where we had just picked up my car. By this time, tractor trailers and automobiles of all kinds went flashing by me. It was very busy do to the extra holiday traffic. I was somehow able to force my car door open, as my husband, thank God was following close behind me.

He was able to follow me directly off the road. Of course, my husband was wondering and not knowing what exactly was taking place. I was able to reach his car. As his window came down, I began to tell him of the distress I was feeling. My husband seeing the anguish on my face thought maybe it was a stroke that I was experiencing. All he heard me saying throughout the experience was "Jesus, Jesus." As I began to pound on the car calling on Jesus to help me; he began to call 911. I could hear him talking to the 911 dispatcher, as he is asking me questions, to relay back to the dispatcher. In between, all I could do is to call only on the one name I knew for help. Oh yes, as I mentioned before, I was born a preacher's kid (PK) through and through. I can strongly without a doubt say I literally have heard the name of Jesus my entire life. So, if nothing else, I knew who, and how to call on his name. Okay back to the story.

"The blood of Jesus, Jesus, Jesus help me." "The blood of Jesus." I repeated not even thinking that this may be it. I was wondering minute by minute, probably second after second where was the ambulance? What was taking it so long? Finally, we saw the flashing lights and heard the siren; unfortunately, coming from the other side of the highway going in the opposite direction. I was in excruciating pain and distress and my husband trying to do his best to calm me down. I heard myself saying, "What in the world is going on?" "Now, this is a pain I have never felt before. Finally, we heard and saw the ambulance making its way to us. When the paramedics arrived, they began to take over and began asking questions of both of us. I tried to answer their questions the best I could in the condition I found myself. I felt myself being lifted and placed into this ambulance all along my mind wondering. *"How did such a beautiful evening come to this."* Leaving my husband behind to follow us. Not really knowing or thinking at the same time that this may be the last time I will ever see him. Luckily, some people may say, but we say by the grace and mercy of God. It was a blessing we were facing in the right direction, less than 15 minutes from Saint Joseph hospital. We were told it was an excellent facility in view of what was taking place with me.

Shortly after arriving, I was alerted that my blood pressure was at an all-time high. My pressure was 200 + / 100 +. Needless to say, I was in such amazement, shock, and confusion because my blood pressure had never been that high before. The doctor on duty informed my husband and I after running several tests that my aorta had ruptured which was connected to my heart. Therefore, I would need to have immediate emergency open heart surgery and the surgeon was on the way. My A-what? I realize now I probably should have paid a little more attention in biology class. It is the main artery of the body supplying oxygen rich blood to the circulatory system. It connects with other major arteries to carry blood away from your heart to the rest of your body: the brain, muscles, and other cells. He continued to explain what all of that entailed. I was having an aortic aneurysm.

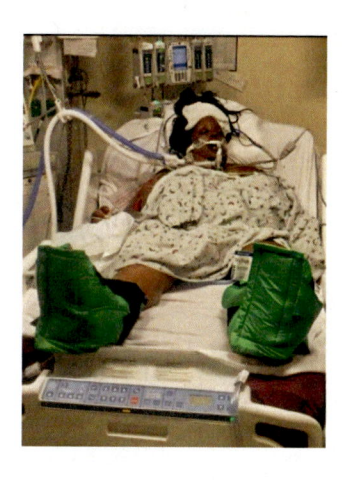

I found myself in a state of disbelief by what was taking place right before my very eyes and what my ears were hearing. My mind was in such a state of unbelief. *"Is this really happening to me right now?"* The pain that initially brought me there had started to calm down and subside. However, numbness and surrealness began to set in with water in my eyes. I remember telling my husband, I have to call my family. Not sure who I would call first to inform them of what had occurred and what was about to take place. A life changing event that I never saw coming. What started out as a relaxing, fun filled evening had suddenly turned into a whirlwind of events beyond my control. After a long night of open-heart surgery; from midnight until the next morning, (7 1/2 hours to be exact), my life would never be the same again. I was later told how my oldest daughter Crystal began to call and started a prayer chain going of people who knew me and loved me. They all came together and began to pray. Thank you God, and to all my prayer warriors out there, thank you.

Fast forward 18 months, I knew some changes had taken place in my body. Always realizing healing was continuing to take place, but all the while feeling something was just not right. I rang the alarm as I call it and discovered a second surgery was needed. Oh boy! Here we go again! Fighting through once again with God's hands on me. I needed another nine-hour surgery this time. It would be a full day after surgery before my eyes would finally open once again to see another day. My family and friends sent prayers up for me continually. I felt equally but perhaps even greater than before that people from far and near had me in their thoughts. Some were aware of the initial surgery period, and now there were others who never knew about my first surgery who were also showing their love, prayers, and unwavering support towards my husband, myself, and my family.

Lord, if you did it before you can do it again! I spent many times thinking; I just know there is light at the end of this tunnel. God/Jesus can you just flicker it a little? And he did! Through a smile of a nurse or an attendant. The light was shown through the voices of my daughters with looks of concerns, but a sparkle of hope in their eyes. The body images of my grandchildren, and just knowing that they were there. From hearing my husband's voice when he came through the door of my hospital room or just holding his hand. To texts that were being sent often from others to inquire about my well-being. Friends and family would also stop by, and receiving phone calls from my sisters who were always praying on my behalf was always uplifting. I began to hear the words of me doing well from the doctors and being moved to a rehabilitation center once again. I thought in my mind another closer step to getting home. It was music to my ears.

This time rehab was in Pennsylvania instead of Maryland. It was much more convenient for my husband to navigate from work and home to see me. It was always challenging for us both, but we never gave up. *"Trust God!"* My husband proclaimed from the beginning with me adding, *"No Matter What!"* Words we both relied on and fought to live by. The light was again beginning to get a little brighter.

I must add here that going through the whole process was such a surreal feeling at times. I really did not understand what others meant when they spoke about having an out of body experience. I am sure it is different for everyone. However, I know now that it can truly exist. Go figure! I thought having a baby was an out of body experience…wow yeah it was. You know you figure one time OK not too bad. The second time just to have something to compare it too. OK, I am done. But three, four, five, six times? God bless you! OK, back to the story at hand.

Throughout this portion of my journey, this just gave me another chance to reflect often on life itself. During my rehabilitation, I found myself in a room with many seniors during our exercise sessions that were well past my age. My heart often went out to them. I extended kind words, a smile at times and definitely prayers. I was able to put life into proper perspective, still having a few challenges of my own, but progressing, nonetheless. I began to understand once again how precious life really is for me.

When we are born, we have a time to live as we get older, then a time to die comes. I was once told the most important time in your life is between your birth date, and the time you die. The dash in the middle is the most important period. What you do with the time in between makes all the difference. However, as we are blessed to get older. Live, live, live every day in your own amazing way.

I left the rehabilitation center, and as I turned into the subdivision of my home, I felt beyond blessed not only for me but for Adrian as well. Seeing the street, the trees, the grass, the neighbors walking throughout the neighborhood. I was finally walking through the doors of my own home; full of a feeling of gratefulness beyond expression. It is extremely hard to describe the sensation that went through my body after being gone for another five to six weeks. Oh, what a feeling! I was still unable to do much. But my rock as he is now known, my husband and my sidekick and my youngest daughter Erica helped to keep everything afloat. During this time, I also had my sister/cousin/friend, Juanita Collick come from Maryland to Pennsylvania to help take care of me which was priceless not only for me but Adrian. He hated having to leave me at times when he went back to work. Also having my daughter Crystal, and the grandkids to visit during the summer (which has become a wonderful tradition for us) was a great help. It was nice having those extra sets of hands in my time of need.

Once again, I was feeling like I was on my way. With my doctor's permission to travel and fly, I attended a wonderful conference with my husband in Charlotte, North Carolina. The expectation and drive to get better was all the motivation I needed to keep me going. The African American Credit Union Coalition, (AACUC) 21st annual conference 2018; my husband would become the Chairman of the Board at that time. While having the most enjoyable experience being there, meanwhile still in the back of my mind plans were being made for my third follow up surgery to be done within the upcoming weeks in August all on the road to a better me. With all that being said, trying to find my new normal to say the least was an incredibly challenging task. But here we are, Wait did you say 4 surgeries. Yes, the last three all within a six-month time frame…and as they say to be continued.

There are several incidents I could share that happened throughout my health challenge. During my many stays at the different hospitals and rehabilitation centers. However, one in particular comes to mind. After having another sharp pain encounter in the middle of the night (at home), unable to bear it. I finally woke up my husband Adrian. He proceeded to call and spoke with my doctor at 2 am. I always teased them and said he and Adrian had a bro-mance going on. Adrian had his cell phone number and could call him at any time. He's the Chief of Cardiac Surgery at the University of Maryland Medical Center. He asked Adrian to take me to the closest hospital where we live in Pennsylvania (York Hospital). After tests were done there, he had them take me to the University of Maryland so he could see me as soon as possible (asap). That didn't happen as fast as we would have liked. He said he could have come and got me himself as long as they took. That's another story. However, the attendants arrived. Secured me in, tied me down in a stretcher and transported me away. Once again leaving my love was a terrifying act. Adrian drove down from Pennsylvania to meet me in Maryland. I was flying through the air with the sound of the propellers from the helicopter. My eyes closed and I was praying all the way.

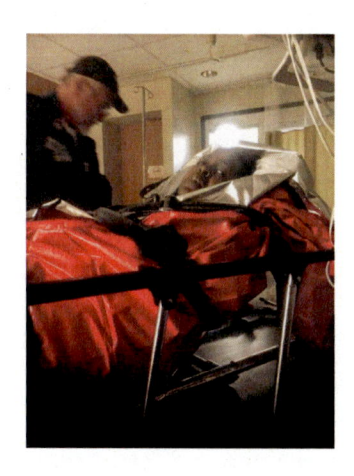

Now, how did I get here? We landed and I was rushed in for more tests. In distress, once more arriving and being tested. Only four days from being there and given the okay, that everything was fine and not to return for the next 6 months. Only to find that I had a leakage now at the bottom of my aorta this time. It is called, a Thoracic Aorta Aneurysm (TAA). The good news is that they didn't have to go through my chest (the surgeons had to do it two times before) and break my chest bones again, but they needed to enter through my side to stop the leaking. I will never forget after receiving the diagnosis of the cause of my pain and discomfort that was delivered from Dr. Bradley Taylor and his team. He didn't even want to part his lips to say what he unfortunately saw and had to be done.

Adrian and I both sitting there with tears in our eyes as he held my hand, trying to take in the realization of a fourth surgery that was needed. It was shocking and beyond belief. Hey God, what's up with this one? I thought we were good. We gathered ourselves, and as we had become accustomed to saying. We have to *"Trust God, No Matter What."* My honey left for the night. It would be a long night of lying there in another hospital room unexpectedly not totally understanding. It wasn't an extreme emergency this time, but the surgery needed to be done before it became one. So it would be a few days lying in the hospital bed before they could schedule me to have surgery once again.

My emotions were at an all-time high. However, in the meantime I had an encounter that calmed my spirit and gave me such peace in the midst of all that was going on. A young lady came by the next day to ask me what I would like for my daily meals. It would be four days before my actual surgery. She saw the anguish I must have had on my face. She asked me if she could pray for me. I said, "Yes, would you please." She came around and put her arms across my shoulders with tears coming down my face, she began to pray for me. After she ended. As anyone who knows me. I proceeded to thank her and ask her name. She said Lorraine. I said wait, what, no way. I told her that was my mother's name who had been gone since 2007. Now, you don't often hear of that name for a younger person. She was about thirty years old. As she left, she said to me, "*It's going to be alright.*"

I felt the peace and the presence of my mom letting me know not to worry. That she was there along with the presence of the Almighty God. I can't explain the calmness and peace I felt. It fills me up and gives me chills just thinking back to it now. My mom used to sing a song in church, entitled, *"I've Got A Feeling That Everything Is Going To Be Alright."* I felt she sent me a sign at one of my lowest times. Hey, call it what you want. I just know, God said, *"Be Strong and Courageous. Do Not Be Afraid or Terrified Because Of Them, For The Lord Your God Goes With You, He Will Never Leave You Nor Forsake You."* (Deuteronomy 31:6) One of Cee Cee Winans songs that helped me through many of my challenging times was, *"Never Have To Be Alone."* Ok, here I go again.

You may want to pause here and go listen. YouTube was my friend. Ok, see. Did you listen? Did you feel it? Well, all I know is that God gave me that sign having my angel to come by who I never saw again throughout all the days I was there. He is sending you signs right now. Remember, you are not alone either and everything is going to be Alright! And as they say…back to the story.

OMG! What in the world now? A pandemic... a Pan... Who? Trying to fight through my own personal quarantine for the past several months which actually has been a two-and-a-half-year journey at this point. Feeling isolated and often alone, I felt myself fighting a greater battle not only physically, but the battle was also taking place in my mind once again. However, I refused to completely shut down inside. I had just been given the go ahead and released from my physical therapy that I had been attending every Tuesday and Thursday mornings for the past ten weeks. The one thing I knew for sure as I stated before, was that my life had changed forever.

Then the following week comes the mandatory shutdown. Were there times when I doubted, I would make it through? Yes! Were my emotions sometimes like a rollercoaster? Up and down! At an all-time high at one minute and down in in the valley the next. Yes, absolutely! Did I want to curse God and die? Are You Crazy!? No! I told God every step of the way, on my hospital bed, at the rehabilitation center, during physical therapy, as well as when I came home even in my personal second quarantine. I told God, asked God, cried even, yes sometimes, I begged God that I wanted to live.

I recalled several times feeling a sensation and a resounding feeling and remembrance of the scripture that states *"You shall live and not die." I shall live and not die, but live to declare the works of the Lord* (Psalms 118:17). Also, as God told Abraham, *"You'll have a long and full life and die a good and peaceful death."* Through faith and the prayers of many, a reassurance calmed my mind and spirit.

Now through the times when I was observing not just what was happening in my own life personally, but really realizing there was so much going on here in the world today. Tensions were at an all-time high. Confusion and cautiousness because of the unknown were filtering through the land, not only here in the states but around the world and all at the same time. I felt and heard that still small voice saying to me *"Stand still and see the salvation of the Lord,"* Exodus 14:13 that scripture would always calm me.

I am sure at the time anyone reads this, we will all be looking back in history. Whether it be for a few months from now or years leading up to this day. We will all know the year 2020, indeed was one for the record books that shifted and changed the world as we knew it. Prayerfully for the better is my hope. Though we are all in the middle of a health shutdown pandemic that is beyond belief.

Although there are several distressing events (pandemic, economic recession, and devastating natural events) that have happened in our world today, racial injustice is once again being brought to the forefront. During the pandemic, we experienced protesting, the looting of small and large businesses, and jobs lost by employees and owners alike. Unfortunately, then there was the death of George Floyd. That changed many things. We sincerely pray that justice will prevail. For a race of people (my race) that is once again sick and tired of being sick and tired. We want true equality. A real healing of the heart and mind, but mostly true and everlasting change. A change in the hearts of men which will look out for the entire human race.

This has left the black community with a floodgate of emotions, questions, and problems. As a result, black Americans have lifted their voices in protest and marched through the streets of our country and across the world. Racism not only exists here in the United States, but throughout the world.

The black community everywhere is calling for a true change and justice with a desire to be heard once again. Unfortunately, there is a lack of sound leadership. There are others who may not understand fully, but are willing to listen and help bring about true change. Sadly, there are some who do not want to listen, and never will understand why we even need change.

While the world was also witnessing record-breaking unemployment on the rise, and destruction, confusion, and chaos all around the globe; I was experiencing my personal health setbacks while these events were happening at the time. As all of this was unfolding, I was asking God to allow me to continue to live.

As time progressed, and a total of six surgeries later, I found myself not as much asking God why any of this happened to me; but asking Him to allow me to continue live. To have more time with the love of my life, Adrian. My attempt to redeem the time we may have felt was lost over the years apart from each other. I wanted to have more time with my sisters Belinda and Diana who have always been there to help me grow in so many amazing ways. I most definitely wanted to have another chance with my two lovely and amazing daughters, Crystal, and Erica. To experience an even greater connection and bond with them and to see all the success and blessings you are bringing into both of their lives. I also had two of the most precious reasons to see my grandchildren, Nilah, and Kingston. To see their lives and goals develop and unfold.

Little did I know my somewhat selfish act of praying and asking Him to grant me more time would result in this one thing. I do know like never before; He has me here for such a time as this. Not only to show you and me but the world in His own way. His power, His love, His compassion, His grace, His mercy, and His kindness and goodness through me. Though once a young little big-eyed black girl who grew up with questions, curiosity, ambition, and a little attitude. Most of the time doing things her own way. Now as an adult, into a big-eyed grateful, thankful, humbled black woman. Ambitious, spontaneous, sometimes stubborn, and still at times doing things her own way. Always loving to laugh with a few tears mixed in as well. Growing up hearing my father preach and my mother singing while playing the piano, *"There is no secret what God can do, what he's done for others, he can do the same for you!"* He has no respect of persons.

This is where I know for me, God has always been in the mix of things. Just like growing through my own personal shut down. He has always been there for me. He said he would be a present help in times of trouble. Also, I will never leave you nor forsake you. You see God and I had history. I can still remember, just looking up at the ceiling in my hospital bed. Wondering several times, God, where are you? You know that human nature part. Repeating the same at home from my bed. Some questions running through the channels of my mind. God, here we are again. My second quarantine, where are you? Realizing it will always be the battle sometimes of the mind and the spirit. "For we wrestle not against flesh and blood but against principalities, against powers..." Where are you? I asked but just like that; then and all throughout my life, God has shown me time after time again, you are never alone. We sometimes forget God's will never override the free will that He gave each of us individually at birth. We so often pray and say, Lord let your will be done then somehow, we do the opposite. But He gave us grace to be in it, and his mercy to see us through it.

I have not worked since the day before Thanksgiving 2017 which has been really weird for me, because I have always been engaged in working since I was a teenager. I felt a personal financial quarantine at times. My husband and my rock has been in a position to provide for me and take care of us, I am forever grateful to him. I can recall the old folks saying, *"God works in mysterious ways."* So, during this time and being shut in, and shut down, creative ideas were flowing; a business being birthed for us, even me writing this for you to read now, and more to come has been a blessing in disguise. Where did the title of this book even come from you may ask? As I have stated before, I've always been a lover of all things beautiful. Whether architecture, fashion, hair, décor of all kinds and even a sunrise and a sunset, etc..

God's creations have always been beautiful to me. But mainly, His creation of people, inside and out. I recall how one day my husband touched my heart in such a way that the title for this book was born. I'll never forget, we both were in our master bathroom just getting ready for the day to attend an event of some kind. I looked of course in the mirror to once again see all the scars left behind from the multiple surgeries I had endured. When sadness came upon me, I made the statement. Wow, look at all these scars. Well, in the midst of me starting to go into my little pity party. And maybe rightfully so. Looking and touching the scars being undeniable. You know, especially for women. As we take pride in our appearance. Okay, call it vanity. He immediately said Babe, I'm not worried about your scars. I'm just glad you're here. It melted my heart in such a way that tears formed in my eyes. And a few days later, the book title came to me.

Beauty Beyond The Scars. Thank you, God. Adrian's words reiterated the blessing I look at each time I walk past a mirror. As a result, from that day since I wear my scars as a badge of honor. We all have them, seen and unseen. Wear them with pride. Remember, if you are reading this you are still here. So, if He brought me through, He will do the same for you!

Quarantine is a period of isolation in which a person or people that have been exposed to an infectious or contagious disease shut down and cease operation. Also, disease is a dis-ease of the body and mind. The process of isolating. The action of detaining someone. The action of confining or state of being confined. However, if you know about quarantine, you must also know the definition of the opposite: Freedom the power or right to act, speak or think as one wants without hindrance or resistance. The state of no longer being in prison or held against your free will, liberated. They can go hand in hand.

So, if you find yourself in your own personal quarantine, whether it be personal, financial, emotional, mental, spiritual, racial, relational, addictions of any kind, etc. or just being afraid or cautious to step outside the box. Take a deep breath and breathe. I can only say this. Yes! I feel as though I have been in my second quarantine, however, truth be told, I may just have been in one all of my life. So, now it is time for you to decide as I had to. Will your life be in constant quarantine, or will YOU emerge with God's help and guidance? Trust God, no matter what, and finally be FREE.

Close Encounters of a Scary Time

In life we all have had scary moments. I have been frightened with death a few times. Once when I was 10 years old I almost drowned while visiting my aunt and uncle in Newark, New Jersey. We were attending the last day of vacation bible school that summer and we went to a popular beach there. I was in the water having a fun time, knowing I had never had a swimming lesson in my life (back then). I was in the ocean when I could no longer feel my footing at the bottom of the ocean floor. Believe me it gives me chills now just as I remember how scared I truly was during this time. I was able to flop, not swim my way back to dry land. I don't think I ever encountered the water again like that until high school where we had a pool and took swimming lessons as apart of PE (physical education). However, I do love the ocean, looking out on it. The peace and serenity it brings but only from a distance now.

My second encounter with death was when I was almost hit by a stray bullet at 19 years old driving home from church with my then baby daughter, Crystal while buckled up in her car seat. This happened before moving to Richmond, Virginia. We were almost home when the back window all of a sudden just shattered. Pieces of glass fell on Crystal everywhere all over the back seat and floor of the car. We drove to my sister's home just around the corner and my brother in law found a bullet shell in the back of the car. All I can say then, and now is "Thank You Lord."

As I mentioned before, my most recent and challenging encounter occurred in November (Black Friday) 2017 emergency Open Heart Surgery. My aorta disrupted. I experienced an Aortic Aneurysm. May 2019 Second Open Heart Surgery for more repair, Sep.2019 3rd Stent placement, Oct. 2019 4th (TAA) leakage Thoracic Aortic Aneurysm. 2021 (5th & 6th) Small Bowel Obstruction Surgery & Internal Bleeding Stoppage.

Facing my biggest health challenge with me having to have emergency open heart surgery in November 2017. I will say has been my most challenging confrontation with death. I was five hours from being rushed to the hospital. I found myself in surgery that would last throughout the night until morning. Seven and a half hours to be exact. For me as you can think, even going back over what occurred back then is a bit challenging. I realize each day what close to death feels like. However, what having life feels like and how precious it is even more to me now.

It is important to understand our precious moments here on earth. We really only have one physical life to live. Life was a gift given to us by God. Whether you believe in the afterlife or not. I pray you do, and get a clear understanding of what that is. Truth be told we all could say we never asked to be here. However, to experience some of the things we all have; the good, the bad, and the sometimes ugly. Many of our relationships, the people, places we all have been and experiences. I can truly say the pleasures of life and experiences I've had; I can never put a price on them. You have to sometimes stop and take a look at how far you've come. Where you are now and look towards the future of what could still be. You also were born for a reason and a purpose on this earth. We can't go back and change much in the past. Unless we are able to go now and try to right some wrongs if we have the power to do so. We can only forge forward to live the rest of our lives as the best of our lives for the future. Why? because you said so, and you have the power to do so. I once read *"As a man thinketh in his heart, so is he."* Proverbs 23:7. Let's get moving.

Family and Friends

In Their Own Words From the Heart

Give an Account of My Illness

Crystal -My First Born/Free Flowing Spirit /You & Me Against the World

      Growing up with the Queen, aka (better known as) Ma! For the first 4.5 years of my life, it was just the Queen and me. A single mother trying her very best to provide, protect, and to love by any means necessary. She will always remind me of the wonderful perseverance that a Queen possesses. She was always striving for the very best for me, even without my biological father present during the early stages of my life. When finding love, my mom graciously included me in the equation, as she married my resilient stepfather whose heart was always to cover us with much prayer and spiritual guidance. He was determined to provide for his family, while exuding unconditional love for his family against all odds. I believe God kept showing proof of my dad's prayers by sending his angels to watch over us.

My mother and I have always shared such an intimate connection because of these reasons. Aside from just being her first born of course, we have always remained very close, even throughout the challenging years of growing pains for me such as adulthood, motherhood, and sudden life changes. My mother holds an extreme special place in my heart that nobody can touch!

Goodness…Ma and I literally cuts up honey! From our 1st, 2nd, and 3rd closing hourly conversations, to remembering coming home every two weeks with my room or the house completely flipped and upgraded with some kind of new home accent, to her undeniable support with preparing and staying committed as a mommy manager/director/opportunist for all of my shows and performances from the start of my entertainment career as a dancer, to hearing my mother sing with such authority and grace, and such sweet melodies to my ears.

Having my mom by my side while giving birth to my beautiful babies meant the world to me. She would send me inspirational messages throughout the years, before social media, cell phones, and pagers. Ma always had a sweet message to share, even on my lunch napkins growing up, I would save each one and store them all in a shoe box that I believe as I think back, helped to strengthen my self confidence that has prepared me throughout my lifetime.

Ma is loads of fun and is always about creating memorable experiences! Growing up watching I LOVE LUCY, 227, The Cosby Show, A Different World, and Nick at Nite in black and white, laid up on the couch underneath one another until I outgrew the sofa and her bed, to working at a very young age inside the hair salons with Ma as a shampoo girl and stylist assistant, and planning and preparing for special events with great fellowship and food are definitely winners for a good time. And for sure, hair moments with Ma always await a fun time, regardless of how you sat in her chair, you most definitely wasn't leaving the same!

As an adult, my mother and my relationship has been a fun filled and beautiful rollercoaster ride that I never want to get off! As with any loving mother, they just only want the best for their child and can only offer the advice or guidance they think would be best for their child's future, right? While life happens in a different space and time, and the child has to experience this thing called life, ultimately by themselves in order to grow and develop into their own identity. Of course, it can cause friction, disappointment at times, a whole lot of prayer for those things beyond our control, which requires pure and unconditional love that only can be expressed from a loving mother and guidance from our creator, God himself. I just thank God every day for my mom continuously because she has been essential for keeping me grounded as a woman, inspired about life, and showing me constantly what real and true love looks and feels like.

Zelda Denise has always been a fireball and ready for whatever because she will always make the absolute best out of any situation. Of course with my mother's sudden heart attack, we all knew this would be an overall life changing experience for everyone. My mother's speed, strength, and endurance was her drive in life. Additionally, her many entrepreneurial ventures, and courage as she not only took care of the family, but also while undergoing several of life's challenges financially, emotionally, and physically health wise. Ma was definitely a mover and a shaker. Currently, she is learning to be skillful at delegating and seems to be becoming a pro at this! When Ma had to retire the scissors and apron after over 25+ years of being a phenomenal cosmetologist, we knew that God had other plans and gifts to activate for my mother.

What!!! Wait…What is going on right now? Were my first words, when receiving the news all at once that my mother was coming from dinner, and she was having chest pains. She was admitted immediately to the emergency room (ER), and they were preparing for an immediate open heart surgery for my mother! Urgently, my mother was requesting to speak with me, and to hear the sound of my mother's nervous, shaking, and afraid voice holding onto to nothing else but her faith that God will see her through; I immediately began quoting scriptures of inspiration, sending reminders of God's love, and praying fervently for my mother to be at peace. I believed God, and whatever the issue was would be fixed totally and completely, and that she would come through victoriously in Jesus name.

I expressed our deepest love for her and that I would look forward to seeing her in a few hours once she returned from surgery. My mother expressed her love for me and her two beautiful grandchildren, Nilah and Kingston, and my mother stated, *"I know God got me!"* I agreed and immediately started to speak with my baby sister Erica, and my Auntie Belinda to gather more of the details and to ensure that they keep me informed of everything, while I was anxiously trying to figure out how I was going to get back home to Baltimore, Maryland to go see about my mother asap! God was bringing it all together, when I received a phone call from one of my mother's lifelong girlfriends, Michelle, who is like an Auntie to me, that blessed me with transportation to go be with my mother, for which I am truly grateful.

In the midst of all of this, God motioned me to STOP EVERYTHING & TO INTERCEDE FOR MY MOTHER NOW! God's voice was so clear and demanding that I felt His authority in welcoming others into a corporate time of prayer and intercession because the word of God says, *"Where there are 2 or 3 gathered in my name, there He is in the midst"* (Matthew 18:20 KJV). We had to go to the throne room on behalf of my mother, and that we did! I created posts on social media, sent texts, and emails inviting all to join in on our designated prayer line and by the end of this prayer call, you could feel that something had shifted in the atmosphere, and we left the prayer call with great expectation that God - Jehovah Rapha was in the room with my mother, doctors, and nurses, as they assisted in keeping my mother's heart beating strong today. Thank you Jesus for every appointed person present in these moments for such a time as this. Victory was won!

Whenever anyone has to undergo immediate surgery for anything it is life changing, especially when pertaining to your heart, blood, and brain functions. It was very difficult to see my mother stretched out in intensive care on a hospital bed plugged up to several beeping machines, and tubes throughout her body; let alone to witness the patch covering my mother's entire chest, where they had to open and repair my mother's heart. Also, during recovery, she had a minor stroke that temporarily paralyzed the left side of her body. While in the room, when I heard of her paralysis, I began without hesitation, rubbing the left side of my mother's body, along with me, and my baby sister. We prayed like never before for my mother's body to be activated, and to come into alignment in Jesus' name. Only minutes later, Jehovah Rapha - God our Healer, showed up right on time, for my mother to wake up out of her slumber to experiencing sudden mobility in the left side of her body. Our God performed a miracle, which confirmed for us that He is ever present; and that's what has given me continued hope in God. He was in control of this matter at hand.

With my mother not only having to undergo (2) major open heart surgeries; she also had to have (2) other surgeries related to her heart and (2) others that were not. They all required a lengthy recovery and healing process. Some had affected her lung capacity and breathing, her stamina, speed, and some areas of mobility have changed. She had six surgeries in total. I remember a little scary moment that happened in the hospital wherein my mother thought (brain irregularities) that she could just get up and go to the bathroom by herself and she ended up on the floor with a minor cut on her head from falling. I quickly advised the hospital staff that more supervision and support would be necessary and that daily activities were in order. Rehabilitation was necessary in order to strengthen lungs, muscles, and brain function, as these certain areas had become weakened due to the shock her body had received. Ma's short term memory was still intact, but she had to reignite some of her long term memory. We were thankful for this, and with this type of transformation, we all learned that it takes time in order for total and complete recovery to happen.

What kept my faith during this experience was believing that my God can and will show up and perform his miracles. God kept showing up in our lives and sending his angels to assist us. God was intervening in every situation; it was evident that my mother was in great hands. My mother has always been resilient and determined in never giving up! My mother is passionate about life and inspiring others on their life's journey. My mother still possesses so many gifts that the world has yet to see, so this is why I believe that God is not finished yet with my mother. My mother is living proof of how sufficient God's grace is, to have spared my mother's life is truly one of my greatest blessings of my lifetime.

Grateful to God, her husband Adrian, my baby sister Erica, and all that has been a blessing thus far within this transformation and throughout. You are greatly appreciated from my heart to yours.

It took many conversations with my heavenly father to keep my mind right, to give me strength to uphold my mother and the rest of the family, and to encourage my mother during her recovery and rehabilitation processes. Being at a distance bothered me a lot because I wanted to ensure my mother had the best care. I wanted her to know that my love and prayers were with her to help heal her heart.

No doubt, this has been an absolute life changing experience for my mother, as well as with her immediate family and close friends. To have witnessed my mother at her most vulnerable state, and to witness her perseverance throughout the stages of rehabilitation, and to intercede for my mother as she had so many times before done for me, strengthened my relationship and intimacy with my creator. To say and know the least, all qualities of a true Queen and Woman of Valor. My mother's life experience has been an awakening within our mother daughter relationship. I am keenly aware of how essential relationships are; especially with being a mother of two, and with knowing that your wealth is your health. It is important for us to take great care of our bodies, to not ignore physical warning signs, and to love hard on your loved ones and close friends, because at any moment, anything is liable to happen. Keeping God first - no matter what for any and all situations. *"Where the spirit of the Lord is, there is Liberty"* (2 Corinthians 3:17). There is unity and there is victory!

KEEP GOD FIRST! We don't have the strength, endurance, or capacity to handle life's challenges on our own. We try it and fail every time when God is not involved in it. God is all powerful, so why not, take the burden off of you and put it in God's hands; and then trust and believe that he will take care of it for you, by any means necessary. Whatever he chooses will be the best choice, because he's still the ultimate creator and everything belongs to Him. He gives it to us, so we can return it back to Him, this way, he can get the glory for the greatness that he predestined and ordained throughout life's experiences.

This is why you must gather in unity, and on one accord, so He can manifest His redemptive power, unconditional love, and grace beyond measure. We should be extremely grateful for God's grace, mercy, love, and favor because we are still breathing and functioning today. Never forget this, it's essential for your life's journey.

RESILIENT - able to withstand or recover quickly from difficult conditions; able to recoil or spring back into shape after bending, stretching, or being compressed. My mother wears this on her crown very well. My mother's inspiration has provided me with my strength, tenacity, and zeal to obtain and ensure the best life experiences for my family and I during this lifetime while here on this earth. Thank you Ma, for even showing your granddaughter Nilah and grandson Kingston how to wear their resilience in their crowns. This is to be treasured and never forgotten, for Victory is her name, aka Ma. Loving you endlessly!

Erica – My Baby, My Songbird – My Flower that Bloomed

Growing up with my mom was a great experience, she's an amazing mom and has always supported me through and through. Some high moments have been her traveling with me to Los Angeles for my first year in college and getting me set up in my dorm room. She would build a luxurious design for my dorm rooms from scratch and bring it to life making me feel right at home. She always put her special touch on everything she did for me. It meant so much to me. Some lows were when I would disappoint her, like the one time I rebelled while on a high school trip that she worked so hard to pay for, and I knew she was disappointed in me; it hurt me to hurt her.

I'm an entertainer, so growing up I would perform and practice for my mom in her bedroom and she would coach me and give me feedback; that's one of my favorite memories we share. Also, one of my mom's many gifts is as an interior decorator, so if I had a long or rough week; when I would come home she would rearrange my whole room around and it meant so much to me. It would make my whole day when she did this.

My mom and I shared many moments but one of my favorite moments was when we would exercise together. We would hold one another accountable while becoming the best versions of ourselves from developing new eating habits to daily workout regimen; there's nothing like it.

My mom is my best friend and mentor at the same time. We have a wonderful relationship, we very rarely bump heads and when we do we talk about it, apologize, and move on. I enjoy our daily talks and laughs. They are the highlight of my day.

My mom is a busy body. Before the procedure she would always be planning and or attending an event, cleaning, and organizing the house decorating and rearranging her home. She was also in network marketing so going to weekly meetings and events was something she always has been committed to, and has excelled in as well. She also is a lover of travel, so she would travel often.

Hearing about my mother's illness was an immediate shock the first time I heard she was sick. It was a double shock when I got the text from my mother's husband saying she's having extreme chest and back pain and is now being flown to the hospital in a helicopter over Baltimore City. All I could do was call some friends and family and prepare myself to go into the hospital and await the doctor's updates as I sat in the waiting area. I did not have too many feelings, I just felt pretty numb.

The medications were my least favorite part of this process because of the side effects. I love holistic and plant based healing techniques. That's something I've noticed as far as a shift in her physicality and energy levels and sleep patterns. Also the pain and healing from the procedure has definitely affected her daily activities and life.

For me, I locked into a daily routine as much as possible. Like working out, eating right, reading, journaling, meditating, and praying etc., to help keep my stress levels down. I also became a health coach and study nutrition to better understand the flow of the body and try to help her more with her recovery and healing process. It definitely made me look in the mirror at myself and my health. And I started to take my well-being more seriously, having heart tests done, locking into nutrition plans, exercising more, and building my spirituality.

When a family member is going through a difficult time like this, it is important to always pour into yourself during this process. It's important to be there for your family or significant other but to not neglect yourself in the process as well. It helps so much. If there was one word to describe your mom throughout this process from beginning to end what would that word be? Warrior is her name!

Juanita Collick – Two Old Souls Connected By Family

My younger years growing-up were adventurous. I was a teenager and Zelda was a few years younger than me. We met after church one Sunday afternoon. My first cousin (Clarence Belton) introduced me to the Lane family. He would talk about his fiancé /soon to be wife, Diana Lane a lot. She is Zelda's second sister, and she would be with her most of the time. We would get together at my aunt's house for Sunday evening dinners, summertime cookouts, birthday parties, etc. Cousin Clarence was what I called him. He loved everything about Diana. Zelda and I would do meet ups at family gatherings, church events, Sunday evening preaching and music church concerts. We always had something to share regarding what was happening in our youth circles and adventures moving forward. We realized during our conversations that we both enjoyed ourselves and talked about doing some of the same things in life. We were always elated to see each other, and it did not matter where and when.

Our bond was like being sisters who lived out of town, and we could not wait to share what was next on our list for having fun. And of course, as of today, Zelda is the youngest best sister cousin friend in my circle of women. I can truly say that over the years she has not changed much regarding our relationship as family, friendship, motherhood, and wifey hood. Zee shared her experience of becoming a Travel Agent and later recruited me as one of her partners with Inteletravel and Plannet Marketing. Zee and I have a lot more fun things on the horizon and I'm looking forward to them all.

Zelda is still the same person that she always was; funny, a health planner, a travel queen, and a stay at home wife. Because of her spiritual walk with Jehovah God, Jesus Christ and the Holy Spirit, things regarding her faith appear to be stronger and more grounded and rooted. She trusted God more; she laughed like a woman with a brand new body of strength. I can't speak to the innermost parts of her anatomy; however, the outermost parts appear to move swiftly through all airports, hotels, restaurants, churches, family gatherings and not sure what's next (LOL). "Trust God no matter what." That's what she and her hubby says.

The prayer warriors were praying nonstop, and Father God honored our prayer of supplication continuously. "What a Mighty God We Serve" Zee does anything and everything she wants to do with no restrictions most of the time, sometimes and we all are feeling sort of aging-in. However, with her new body parts, she has not missed a beat when it comes to getting out of the home and going to the "Ravens Game." (LOL) Some of us in the past would talk about giving the drummer some. How about giving God the highest praise, hallelujah. Truly, wonderful is His Name forever and ever. God knows best, and He set us all up to bear witness of his goodness and miraculous show out.

I am grateful to have shared Zee's body and mind transformation. For me only, I think it made Zee stronger, and more fearless to continue on her journey of life. Because the prayers of the righteous availeth much. James 5:16. True believers never give up; we just hold on. Our relationship means as much to God the Father as it means to us his children.

Zee's situation changed me in many ways. I trust more, believe more, and I am more patient in waiting on God. I pray more, and laugh more. I only allow believers in Father God around and pray for others daily. It's important to understand that I am going to pray, don't worry. Stand on the word of God and trust him with all of your heart and might. Praying and asking Father God to send you prayer warriors daily.

One word to describe my friend is *Resilient*. Zelda is my sister/cousin/friend . I always tell her that she is like a cat and has more than nine lives. She can come through any situation and land on her feet and take off running. What a mighty GOD we serve. I have learned to trust God's words, and I stand on His promises according to what He says. I believe Him only and I wait patiently for His answers. Remember, we should lean not to your own understanding, in all your ways acknowledge Him, and he shall direct your path. Proverbs 3:6.

Michele Ellis-Williams – Near or Far – My Sister Friend Until the End

Initially I met Zelda relocating to Atlanta from Maryland by a friend who owned a performing arts school next door. Zelda's two daughters attended there. One of her daughters was a student, and the other an occasional dance instructor, which gave us an opportunity to see each other often. Zelda and I immediately became friends due to the love of interior design. Her eye for design and beautiful decor allowed our relationship to evolve. As a result, our friendship morphed into a work relationship. Zelda became my top interior decorator. She and I worked together for years enriching the lives of others by enhancing their personal spaces.

I remember Zelda as a kind gentle person with a heart to serve others. As a matter of fact, Zelda was so awesome that many of my clients would request to work with her because she was so talented, personable, and they loved her personality. Unfortunately, I found out that she was ill through a mutual friend Venetia. She called me and asked, "Did you hear about Zelda." I said, "No," and she said that Zelda was rushed to the ER. I literally freaked out and called Zelda's daughter right away. I requested that my husband book me a flight to Maryland ASAP! Honestly, nothing else mattered at the moment, and my heart was beating so fast! I felt like I had to get to my friend right away by any means possible. However, I realized that it was more important that her daughter Crystal, who was living in Atlanta, be by her mom's bedside. Crystal had promised to keep me abreast of Zelda's health status. I prayed for Zelda during this difficult time, but I did not worry. I knew Zelda had faith in God and would be fine. I also knew that she had a strong network in her family and especially with her husband Adrian. Although I did not get to see Zelda when she was ill; her daughters kept me updated on her condition. Zelda had the same spirit I had grown to love when I spoke to her, so it was difficult to tell that she was ill. She simply sounded weak.

I am overjoyed and thankful that Zelda is doing well. We all must live each day to the fullest. Make certain that you have your affairs in order. Additionally, it is important to give those you care about their flowers while they are here on earth. Take advantage of every moment life gives to you, and do not sacrifice your health. Strive to live a healthier life by eating right, exercising, and most importantly being spiritually grounded. Lastly, secure your circle with individuals that truly have your back!

My Dear Friend - Renée Sattiewhite – Sagittarius Sister Connection

One of my favorite memories is when she wanted to surprise her husband on his birthday, and we created a birthday book for him. He never knew we were plotting on surprising him.

Another consistent memory is Zelda and her husband get up early in the morning and fellowship – ever so often I would call on a Saturday morning and talk to the both of them on speaker phone.

I met Zelda through her husband Adrian. If you ever talk to Adrian and he starts talking about his amazing Zelda – his eyes light up and you can tell his heart is bursting with love for her. I was happy to meet the lady who had captured his heart so very long ago. I am always inspired by great love stories, and they have one. When Adrian was the Chairman of the Board of the award winning African American Credit Union Coalition (AACUC), I would refer to Zelda as "First Lady." She was thoughtful, caring, and charismatic and always treated me with kindness.

When I found out about Zelda's illness, I went into high gear praying. I wanted to do something to keep her spirits up while she was in the hospital, so I crocheted her a blanket and gave her a book to read with a title of "First Lady." I would check on Adrian and her regularly. Initially, when Zelda was diagnosed, of course there was a change in how she was able to move around – but I would say that her spirit got even stronger, her faith is immeasurable, and I believe she sees her tests as great testimony to the power of prayer and God's grace.

I believed Zelda would recover because she didn't have a choice. Too many believers praying for her and her relationship with God. I also believe that her relationship with Adrian was her lifeline and motivation. Their love is strong. I prayed for my friend when she was ill, and her illness has changed me in that I have become more deliberate about taking care of me spiritually and physically. I would recommend that anyone who is ill would get prayer warriors together. Set up a support system and listen to the doctors.

Resilient is the word to describe my friend, and when I spoke to God about her situation, I felt full of hope and certainty that she was going to be OK.

Diana Belton, Sister – My Sister and Prayer Warrior

My baby sister the one I love so much. Surprising to know that we are 12 years apart. My older sister and I never knew that we would be the babysitter, but never was she difficult to watch. One of the fondest memories was when we went to Indiana on a bus trip using the money I had from a car accident. We did a lot of fun things especially going on church trips to the amusement parks. We were very close especially after my oldest sister left home and was no longer with us. We always covered for each other up to the time I got married. She cried to go with me on my honeymoon. She just couldn't understand why she couldn't go.

My sister was a get up and go person, nothing seemed to stand in her way. The day before she was diagnosed; she and her husband were here in Baltimore sitting at my son Terrance's table having Thanksgiving dinner. Zelda was always working. She was either doing hair or learning more about her passion as an interior decorator.

My immediate reaction was to call on my God, the one and only one that knew what was happening. My niece Crystal instantly put together a group text and we all went in prayer touching and agreeing on the phone. Her diagnosis was shocking, but we knew God was able to heal her. I can tell she became more fearful, but still playful. When God allowed her to know this sickness is not unto death. By his stripes she will be healed. I believe one of the strips was her recovery.

I continue to pray and pray and be there for her and her husband. I knew that our mother and father both had heart problems. It caused me to continue to pray and keep looking out for the rest of us. Don't take things for granted, especially your body. And then I would have to give them my sister's testimony to let them know what God is able to do. The one word that I would use to describe her is "Faith."

GOD has given us permission to obey him at his word. So I just started quoting exactly what his word said concerning his children.

Isaiah 65:24 (NKJV)

Again, truly I tell you that if two of you are on earth agree about anything they ask for, it will be done for them by my father in heaven.

Matthew 18:19 (KJV)

Belinda M. Lane, Sister - My Confidant & Cheerleader (Mother/Sister/BFF)

Zelda and I shared most of our adult life together. To be totally honest we never argued. When we had disagreements, we would choose to agree or to disagree and kept it moving. We always knew we had each other's back without ever having to verbalize it.

The only lows were when I left home, and she was almost 4. I was concerned about what she was told and how she would understand why I was no longer in the home. Because I took care of her and my brother as if they were my children, leaving my siblings behind was very painful.

Zelda always seemed to be a happy child. She was a child humanitarian. I believe this incident happened before she started school. I can recall that she saw a little girl in a magazine crying and asked my mother why the little girl was crying. My mother told her it was because she was hungry. It was a "Care Project" advertisement. Zelda put together a puppet show in our backyard and charged the neighborhood children to attend. She took the money from the show and gave it to our mother and told her to send it to the little girl in the magazine. She hasn't changed.

When Living in Georgia…

- Once we reconnected, we would go see new homes and always went to the "Street of Dreams" showroom
- We did network marketing together and met some amazing people and traveled with them to conferences and conventions all across the country and internationally
- We never get tired of talking to each other
- I would take her to the circus
- Traveled together

We are very close! Basically for the 1st 3 ½ years of her life. She was more like my child than sister. Before Zelda's diagnosis she was, always outgoing, she loved people and again she always wanted people to succeed in life… a real humanitarian. When I found out she was ill, I was devastated and immediately headed for Maryland praying all the way. I don't believe she ever took life for granted. She became more intentional. She was always a good person, and optimistic. She may have started to feel a little more sense of urgency about life. I believe my sister was a fighter. I never believed it was her time to go, never!

We prayed for her. My sister, Diana and I fasted as well and believed God. I also knew she was in good hands regarding her husband and his love for her would cause her to fight and live. I decided to be at peace. I did not change. I made a decision to trust God for her healing.

My sister was very encouraging!!! She had her vision boards at the hospital and was also encouraging the hospital staff. Other words to describe my sister are; optimistic, relentless, a visionary, and challeng-ing. When Zelda was ill, she and I had very positive conversations. We believed God was going to work everything out and He did. I know it sounds simple; but quite literally, it was just simply a decision to believe. Simply … to trust God! No, it may not be as easy as it sounds. But it is a choice!

♡ **Adrian- My Loving Honey!**

I met my wife at a dance at Morgan State University back in May of 1979. Her high school Dunbar (in Baltimore, Maryland) was having their Spring Dance. In the fall of 1979, she would be entering the 11th grade. We saw each other almost every day for about six months before she abruptly broke off our relationship. I was devastated! I was a loyal boyfriend. I thought we enjoyed spending time together. At the time she did not have a license. So, I would pick her up from wherever, and we would go shopping, or go to the movies, or get something to eat. Sometimes we would hang over her oldest sister's house or a friend's house, or even my house. My wife and I are both the youngest in our family, the babies. We have a special bond because of that. She is the artsy person, while I'm the numbers guy, but we both have a great sense of humor. Oh, yeah, we both love to laugh! Although, we are both loving, caring, compassionate, (but at this age) purpose driven people. In addition, we enjoy going to sporting events, movies, comedy, and jazz shows. We watch documentaries, fine dining and enjoy the arts and both music and plays. In fact, we travel well together as we enjoy different places and each other's company. Sometimes when discussing an issue or topic, we also agree to disagree. Nevertheless, we keep it moving and don't let it negatively impact our relationship. For the most part, every Friday is date night. Something we both look forward to.

My wife was full of energy. She took care of our house, and she was very creative. She has major interior decorator skills, and her skills are amazing! We have a beautiful home. So when everything started happening, I was in a state of confusion. This thing happened so quickly. I just could not grasp what was happening at the time. How do we go from dinner with friends to emergency Open Heart Surgery in a matter of 6 hours? It was unbelievable! My wife still has health challenges she did not have before. She can't do some of the things she could do previously. We truly have to pace ourselves. It all has forced me to help out even more.

In spite of some fearful times, I believe my wife would recover because of Faith! I would ask God to show me a sign. As far as I can remember, upon that request the results were always positive. Keep in mind, though, my wife is still recovering and learning more about her body, but getting stronger each day. At times when things were happening, I cried a lot and prayed a lot. I ultimately decided to keep the faith and remain hopeful and optimistic. I looked at the big picture. I started listening to gospel music daily. I found it calms me. I also made a decision to pay her bills to make sure her credit would not be negatively impacted. It made me realize what is important.

Now, I try to spend as much time as I can with her. We celebrate the first day of every month as our anniversary. January 1, 2023 was 72 months(6 years) Ultimately, I hope when faced with such a challenge in your life you would seek some help and guidance to deal with such a situation. I am talking about professional help! You have to communicate what you are experiencing. Get it out! Even though we had not made it to 11 months of marriage yet. My prayer was, "Please do not let her die (on me). We have too many good things to do and accomplish together.

She is resilient! You know God gives his toughest battles to his strongest soldiers. Our wedding (marriage) vows ring true; "for better or worse, and in sickness and in health, for richer or poorer." Our faith and our favorite saying is…"Trust God, No Matter What!"

Chapter 4

Beautiful Words of Wisdom

Secrets to a successful marriage

Of course I am not an expert when it comes to marriage. However, I have learned that there are a few things one can employ to have a successful marriage. First, it is important to be honest and trustworthy. This is huge in a relationship. We often underestimate the power of honesty and trust. Second, it is critical to be respectful at all times. Third, a couple should be open with each other as much as possible. It may not always feel good, but it's needed. Fourth, I have found that working together and having each other's back will make a serious difference in the relationship. In addition to always taking time with one another is a factor that we often forget. I believe it is important to learn one another's respective roles in the marriage; both individually and together. According to Gary Chapman, you should know each other's *"Love Language."* The five love languages that he outlines are: receiving gifts, words of affirmation, quality time, acts of service, and physical touch. Just know that love is a choice. Since each person was raised differently, you may have a lot in common that we bring together to the table. However, there are things and ways you don't that can tear you apart. You must be willing to acknowledge the issues and address your concerns. If not, it can only lead to disaster. How will you go forward with the differences that you may face? We must also learn not to take everything so personal. Just for that reason. Because along with our similarities we're all so different. Our perspectives are different, our thought processes may not be the same. That's where that respect comes in again. I may not agree with you, but I can respect your point of view. That can go a long way. We must agree to disagree. Oh, and by all means have as much fun as you can with each other.

Finally, a couple must trust God, then trust yourself. (OK I sound like my mom).

I believe that doing both will yield you whatever you desire. I don't want to sound like this should be the last resort, it actually should be number one and throughout. God gives us instincts and we must use them. I am encouraging others don't forget to do the same for yourself. It's easy for me to tell others how intentional I am about me. Because I have discovered what I've been placed here to do on my life's journey. In order to have a successful relationship, we must learn to love, be kind, and appreciate others in life, just like we want to be treated. We are all only human. No one is supernatural or perfect but God. I also have to remember even God rested. I do have to take care of myself as I continue to live my life. You must give yourself grace as well!

I just had the pleasure of witnessing my husband, Adrian Johnson being inducted into the African American Credit Union Coalition (AACUC) Hall of Fame while celebrating the 25th Anniversary of the organization at Stone Mountain in Atlanta, Georgia. He was presented an award for his contributions to the AACUC and financial industry for 45 years of service. I also wanted to honor all the love, support, and care he had shown and given to me during our journey especially these past 6 1/2 years that we have been married. As I have often stated, he's been my rock and Dwayne Johnson Hollywood's rock doesn't have anything on him. I wanted to present him with a special honor at the 25th anniversary of the AACUC when he was the chairman for the organization from 2018-2020. So much was going on at that time. The Covid pandemic, George Floyd, along with the Black Lives Matter movement and then caring for me. I have so much respect for caregivers, it's never easy. So, I presented him with an award of love and appreciation on the last day of the conference which read: **YOU ARE MY ROCK, ALWAYS MY ANCHOR, TODAY YOU ARE MY WORLD!** No words will ever express my heartfelt gratitude towards you, Adrian "**My Rock Johnson**" you said it best during your acceptance speech. "For better or worse, richer, or poorer, in sickness and in health." It's amazing that we have each other. Thank You!

AACUC 2023

Dealing with Adversity – A Game Changer

Wow, we all face adversity, I'm sure on different occasions. Weekly, if not sometimes daily, I have considered myself a fairly positive person for as long as I can remember. I attempt not to look now so much at the person as to look at what is even causing the negative behavior. I had a past associate minister at my former church in Virginia teach me something that I will always remember. He said, "You must always go to the root of any problem, situation, or encounter with people to try and understand how it started **and possibly the cause of whatever it may be.**" There were times in my younger years I may have gotten upset. I have never been a confrontational person. I never liked drama. However again being the baby of my family, I always spoke my peace still until this day. I try to see each side of a situation. Knowing it may be my side, your side, but ultimately for me what is God's side.

I along with my husband are very protective of our space and our peace. I have recognized in my latter years how I have taken on the personality, disposition, and spirit of my mom. She would, "Kill you with kindness" so to speak. My siblings and I laugh how she would love you, talk with you, but would get you indirectly without you even knowing you were being gotten (excuse my wording). She just had a way. I miss that. My dad on the other hand can be kind in his own way but would be stubborn as well. I'm told I have the characteristics of the two. However, he stood his ground. You may have been upset and felt a little negatively in some way. But you knew for the most part it was all for your good. So, I find myself learning and agreeing to disagree. Because everyone is truly different. There's a book I read called "The Four Agreements." It speaks to our upbringing and all what we may have learned in our developmental process. Our foundation and principles that were good and necessary. However, I do feel that the world we live in is ever changing. Our message doesn't have to change but sometimes our methods have too (i.e., the way we do things).

This world is just made up that way. Even though I believe God created us all. He also created us differently in our own way. We all have to recognize that. When we don't we will always continue to see things and people in a negative way. My sister and I have a saying, "Sometimes you just have to love people from afar." This includes family, friends, coworkers etc.. In the end, as Kenny Rogers said, "You got to know when to hold them, know when to fold them, know when to walk away, know when to run." Not just with cards and money but with people too.

Parents and Communities:

Let's Work Together

I was asked about the state of our children today as compared to the days of our upbringing. As a child for the most part, our parents, along with our grandparents, some aunts, uncles, teachers, etc. trained us to the best of their ability. They trained us directly and indirectly. I used to say my mom would kill you with kindness. You were being got when you didn't even know it. I was being trained. I feel that in this day and time we have to be very direct and intentional with our children. There is so much more competing for their attention. Yes, we may have had TV at times and a home phone that was to be used in a limited fashion. We also had fewer places to visit and less entertainment in general, however, we made it through by the grace of God.

Our children these days are faced with far more than we ever had to handle. However, I realize that each generation has had its challenges. Now, this generation has to deal with exposure to computers, social media, cell phones at your fingertips, and cable streaming television 24 hours a day, seven days a week. Yes, we can limit them. As parents, we may intervene and take devices from them which may help to reduce some of their intake. But to be real and true, it's constantly all around them 24/7. I believe we should train them that this is the world we live in, but as the Bible teaches us, "We are in the world, but not of the world." Meaning you have a choice. You don't have to go along with everything you see, hear, or touch in the world. I believe we should train our children in Proverbs, the wisdom book. If anything, it teaches all of us, even adults, the way in which to think, make decisions and grow in life. We as adults must continue to help build a good foundation. I don't believe it's too late.

Today, we often hear the following sayings: "It Takes a Village," "Our Tribe," and "Our Crew." Whatever the term may be, we need to work together. We should have parental opportunities throughout each community, city, and state to help with the raising and parenting of our children to better the world we all live in today. In reality, none of us asked to be here. It was all God's plan. However, He has entrusted us with the children brought into this world and to help each other. Therefore, it is up to us to "Train up a child in the way he should go, and when he/she is old they will not depart from it." Proverbs 22:6. Or can I say far from it. We also need to place God back in the schools. I feel a lot of what is happening may not have happened if God was never taken out of schools. We must institute the ten commandments, prayer, and other forms of godly behavior in our homes and in our churches; even if they never place it back in the school system. Children need more attention than we tend to give at times. Here are a few things we can do to help our children:

- A weekly check in period.
- A goal and purpose list to go over every 2 to 3 months to keep them on track in different areas of their lives.
- Reward and acknowledge them when things are good. Confront and acknowledge them when things are not so good.
- Unless we take time as adults and parents to put some things in place we have nothing but their own behavior good or bad.

In spite of what's going on in all of our adult lives. We must be present intentionally in our kids', teens, and young people's lives. Often I say, "Truth be told." They didn't ask to be here. None of us did. However, I believe everyone and that means you too are a gift. Let's be a gift to our children as we continue to be a gift to each other. Again, yes we praise them for the good. Correct them in the bad. Help guide them when they are stuck. We've all been through it before ourselves. Whether we had someone there for us or not. There are some things they may need to figure out. But how about a little more help with the things that they really do need help with; like finances, and how to manage them. Relationships that always feel good to you aren't always right for you. Friends, opposite sex, jobs, leisure time etc.. It's all a part of life and the growth process. Why do we neglect it so? I believe unfortunately our kids' world has been adjusted. Yes let kids be kids, but we should be preparing them for the future. The world is so different now from when we were kids.

We have to start equipping our children that way. If not, so many will be left behind. I stated before that our morals, foundation, principles, and messages should or may not change but our methods may have to in order to reach our children today. Our phones are no longer rotary or attached to the wall. Now we carry them in our pockets, in our hands, and on our arms. However, the message we communicate is still the same. Hello, is still "hello" and "goodbye "is still goodbye. If you get the picture.

We need to talk and have real conversations with our children. As adults, I believe we give them many excuses. "They don't listen. There are so many things vying for our kids and young people's attention. Believe it or not, as parents, grandparents, teachers, leaders etc., we are in competition with all the outside distractions. How many times have we told our children they are leaders when we are not truly trying to lead them? It becomes a figure it out game as many of us have experienced in our own lives. It's time to change the narrative for our children. If we don't, just know that the world and all its ideas will. We have to make our children a priority.

Seek out their gifts, talent, intelligence, creativity, their wit. etc.. Ultimately, what they may bring to their life and the world. Always to be respectful. However, the children are to be seen and not heard theory I believe it's long gone. We have to find ways to continually have conversations; and be engaged with them and their futures. Being serious when needed but also having fun in-between.

Community Relationships – No Man is an Island

There is no question that our communities need to be rebuilt. I believe there are ways to right some of the wrongs in our community. We must be willing to provide everyone with the basic necessities of life such as housing, food, clothing, transportation. People within communities must obtain a decent job at a decent wage. The cost of living keeps going up drastically, and wages should be moving up to reflect the cost of living increase. We should all desire to live comfortably. We should also create recreation centers and community buildings in all neighborhoods for education such as mentoring programs, job fairs, social activities, and enjoyment purposes.

Law enforcement and the community should always work together to address the negative aspects of our society as well as participate in the neighborhood activities to create positive opportunities as well. We should also have an overhaul of the criminal justice system. To be fair to everyone. Some laws need to be changed and done away with in order that things are equal for everyone.

To limit or not limit social media. It can be good and not so good. Advantages along with disadvantages. Children need to be aware of the company they keep. The sources of influence. I used to hear "The saying birds of a feather flock together." My parents would constantly teach us to be aware of our surroundings and teaching us who to run with and who to associate with and who to connect and disconnect with. I believe that there is not enough adult attention and intention in their lives. Children need more attention than we tend to give.

A New Outlook – Health is Wealth

Because I have experienced quite a bit in the past several years regarding my health, it has become one of the priorities in my life. If we could turn back time, I'm sure that we all would change some aspect of our health. My major challenge has been consistency. Understanding in order to get the results I want I must be intentional about my health. I have to have a true lifestyle change. Old ways have brought me to where I was in the past. New ways are helping to bring me to a better way of living now and for the future. I had to believe first, and then take control of me. Because faith without works is dead. I have to do the work. There's no getting around it. I did find out when you surrender and focus, then God gives you the strength to do it. I honestly feel as though my health ultimately did not have to come to this point. However, God is the God of a second, third, fourth, and so on chances and for that I am truly grateful. Most importantly, it is written in His word and our blueprint is given. We must stop ignoring the instructions. We hear, and we hear, myself included, but when will we actually act on the knowledge that has been given in regard to our health, fitness, and our overall wellbeing? His mercy does endure forever, but our bodies would be much better if it were in alignment with his grace. We simply must take better care of them. Ok, Zelda here's that advice you also must take.

To maintain my health requires a lot of prayer and so many are praying for me. I have to then remind myself constantly that my body is my temple and a gift from God. What goes in it, and what I do to it really matters. So I try to intentionally do things to strengthen my body such as eat things that nourish my body and my mind as well. I believe that is the key. At least for me, I once heard one of my very smart and direct mentors MG, state that the one subject that is the least taught or even spoken of from the Bible is on gluttony. Everything else we can be condemned for, criticized, damn to hell, but not gluttony! And it's the number one cause of so many sicknesses and diseases that occur by what we're putting into our bodies on a continual basis. There was another young lady in a documentary I saw called *Feel Rich*, she stated as she had just finished burying and putting her aunt in the ground at her funeral just to come back to the repass to eat some of the same foods that helped put her aunt in the ground in the first place. Please just ponder on that for a while! Guilt! OK, Zelda move on!

It's not always easy but I do believe I have become better and more conscious then I have been in the past. By doing so I truly believe God honors that. I realize my body is only temporary, however; I must take care of it daily. My body and health are a gift. My life is a gift. I must unwrap it and use it wisely.

There are several things I do believe that we should all be focused on that will take us through life. Proverbs, as I said before is one of my husband's and my greatest and favorite book in the Bible. Instead of us all just trying to figure it out. It is full of so much wisdom and direction even when it comes to our health.

Our Health

How we should understand the proper way to nourish our bodies and our minds. Along with keeping active. A little bit each day of movement. I know it can be challenging at times. It is or me. My weight can fluctuate up and down, back and forth. However, I can't quit, you can't quit. Your health and life depends on it. As Michael Jackson (MJ) would say, "I'm talking to that man in the mirror, I'm asking him to change his ways." OK you know I had to say it!

Our Wealth

Knowing how to understand and manage money and credit. To live day-to-day and prepare us for the future, we must take the time to learn how money can enhance our lives and legacy and not to be afraid of what we don't quite understand. Be intentional to get the knowledge needed to stop living from paycheck to paycheck, and really acquire wealth. As my husband, Adrian Johnson states, "If there is not a millionaire in your family, create one."

Healthy Relationships of All Kinds

These relationships should be of all kinds (boyfriend & girlfriend, husband & wives, mother & father, daughters, sons, siblings to siblings, family to family, neighbor to neighbor, employee to employee, employer to employee etc.). We should all be getting wisdom and understanding. I believe living by these principles will help us journey positively through this life. This in turn will prevent so much stress, heartache, and division. I believe in educating and executing to bring us all closer together.

I often quote when God said to Moses. *"What is that you have in your hand"?* Use It! It was his staff. We often continue to look outside of ourselves instead of what he has already given us, and supplied us with. Somehow we forget to use it. He said everything pertaining to life He's given us. It's right there inside of all of us.

A Living Legacy

It is important that we leave words of wisdom for our children. I wish to give my children and grandchildren a heads up in life. It will save them a few heartaches and headaches. These are principles I have always taught them throughout their life. First, always put God first intentionally. My children should actively read and live the book of Proverbs because it will give them all the knowledge and wisdom they need to make it through this life. I wish I had locked myself into Proverbs much earlier. Understand and realize this is a crucial part of our road map for life. It will save you a few heartaches. Any of my assets will be given to my girls. Crystal, Erica and my grandchildren Nilah and Kingston. Along with my husband Adrian who will be in charge of it all. I want my children to be an example of goodness as I hope I have been. Most importantly, I leave them my laughter, contentment, joy, creativity, and happiness and my unwavering love for God.

In the end my legacy should focus on these three points:

1. That I was a kind and loving person.
2. That I made life and experiences better for my husband, family, and friends.
3. That for the majority of my life I tried to see and address life in a positive way. Like my mother, I lived my life as if I never met a stranger.

Specifically, I incorporate all these guiding principles in life in these daily ways.

1. Usually, I do get up early. Sometimes earlier than most at 3,4 or 5:30 a.m.

2. I have a cup of coffee or tea.

3. Do some early morning chores and household messing around.

4. I have my devotion time and I use my awesome Bible App (which feeds my spirit and my soul).

5. If my husband is working from home or going into work, I always prepare my husband's lunch and snacks for the day. I always leave him a positive handwritten note on his napkin each day just so he knows how much I love and appreciate him. I do this to encourage and express my ultimate love to him throughout the day. We must not take anything for granted. Ok, I know we sound pitiful, but it works for us.

6. We drink our Tahitian Noni juice religiously every day to keep our immune system stronger.

7. Attempt to get my thoughts and tasks down of what I would like my day to look like.

8. I always get ready depending on my agenda for the day.

*Over the past few years I've had to alter some of my routine according to several doctor's appointments and procedures in regard to my health.

- I like to read or listen to positive and informative speakers through audio messages. OK! I am a YOUTUBER.
(Myron Golden, Myles Monroe, Les Brown, Eric Thomas, Joel Osteen, T.D. Jakes, Lisa Nickles, Jim Rhon, Zig Zeigler, Oprah Winfrey, Steve Harvey) just to name a few of my favorites.
- Talk to my sisters/daughters and a few close friends daily.
- Prepare dinner possibly three times a week.
- Enjoy watching programs daily with my husband. Some we taped to watch during later times. Ex: *Saturday Morning, *Sunday Morning, *60 Minute, *Dateline,* American Greed, *World News Tonight with Lester Holt are some of our rituals. We also love documentaries, sports, and a special movie of choice. Let's not forget HGTV and all of my judge shows. Date night each Friday night which is our weekly event. We look forward to this night. There are times that we have a nice evening at home together or venture out of the house. That is our special time.

In the end, I think we all need to have more fun in our lives. Here are some of the things that I do for fun:

1. Being with my husband
2. Travel (My husband and I really enjoy traveling together).
3. Attending sporting events, plays, the theater, orchestra & jazz concerts
4. Dining out (experiencing different restaurants).
5. Enjoying family & good close friends
6. Watching funny comedies, romantic movies, old movies, and decorating shows (all day). Ok, maybe not all day. One thing is for sure they all bring me joy. We also love documentaries (usually any historical segments, sports, and special programs. Also, as stated, I enjoy all of my judge shows. Ok, I had a long time to recover. Television became my alternate friend.
7. Talking to good friends (past & present) It energizes me, encourages me, and often inspires me. I am a firm believer that "Iron Sharpens Iron"!

Also, that "Laughter Does A Heart Good Like Medicine." Proverbs 17:22. I come from a laughing family and my life has had its share of pain, but laughter, fun and joyful experiences has always brought me through.

Rededicating Our Lives to Christ

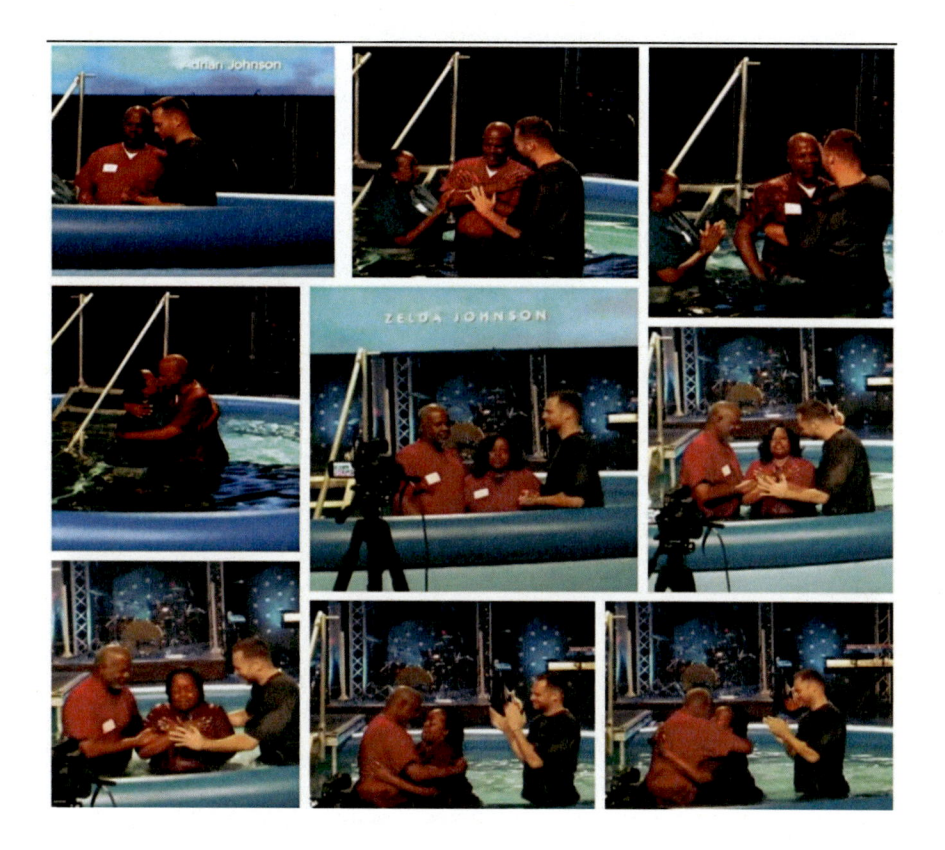

Baptism My Significance:

It is not just what God has taken me through, it's all about what he is taking me to. You and I are here for a special reason. I found that in the midst of chaos, it can feel like you don't have God's attention. However, the truth is, I and you were chosen. God has covered and protected me all my life. There is more that God has for each of us. Deep inside I know you sense it too. There is more that God has for you. I found the obstacles of my past have been training me for something greater and higher. Never think that God has abandoned you. God has always had my back and He has yours. It's time to disrupt the narrative. That is trying to discard or discourage you in any way. You and I are needed here as never before. As you can see, I chose to "Trust God No Matter What" by doing a public display of His presence in my life.

I remember being baptized at the age of five years old by my father. I held him so tightly around his neck with my little legs wrapped around his waist as he dipped me in the baptism pool with his white robe flowing in the water. I think back now as I am crying writing this. That was actually the beginning of my connection to my faith in God. I know my father said I got you. Just like I had to trust my father here on earth. I had to learn to trust my heavenly father as well.

Throughout my life's journey. I went on to get baptized once again at the age of 35 at my church. When I attended Destiny Metropolitan Worship Church in Atlanta. Even though I was so young when I first was baptized by my dad. I felt that by being older I was showing (an outward demonstration) of my faith and public acknowledgement. It brought me joy to once again do so.

Fast forward to November 2018. My church, Lives Changed By Christ (LCBC) here in Pennsylvania has baptism every quarter. And after witnessing my husband Adrian being baptized in 2017 for the first time, the year prior. It warmed my heart and I felt so proud of him. I started to entertain the thought of all I had been through. I felt being baptized this time was like a rebirth, leaving it all behind. A second chance at life with family and close friends in attendance to celebrate with me it was such a joyous experience. Remember God's unfailing love. He knows your name and you are significant to Him.

The End...Or Just The Beginning

Being a new author and just figuring out this whole writing thing; I am hoping that just reading and taking this journey with me to hear a piece of my story will inspire you in some way. Hopefully, you will be more intentional about your life, and know that it's never too late to change the direction of your story and to continue to make progress on the path you are on now.

By reading my story, my hope is that you are able to relate to the many twists and turns in my life. My hope is that you heard and felt my heart (No pun intended). We all have a short time here on this earth together. Let's make it count. Enjoy the experiences along the way. We often desire things, people, situations etc. to come in nice, neat packages that we can digest and unwrap easily. Life lessons are what I call them. They come in many forms. It's up to us to accept or sometimes reject it. Some things we can't control, others we can just by the decisions we make. Remember again, "As A Man Thinketh So Is He." There are so many sayings and clichés, and affirmations out here that we have chosen to listen, repeat and even live by. Consciously or unconsciously. Some were passed down and taught. Some have shaped our lives and continue to do so. I've shared a few of my favorites I hope you will enjoy and embrace. That they may encourage you whenever needed. I pray that you have more triumphs than traumas in every area of your life.

I believe no one truly knows but God. I found myself seeking Him with my whole heart, listening to and following His lead. I found life to be so much better that way. Not always making the best or always right decisions, but doing the best at what I have been given and created to do. As I stated before. This life comes with so many twists and turns. I found twisting and turning with my Heavenly Creator makes navigating through life a little easier.

I employ you to do this. Sit back and take a deep breath. Use this moment to reflect back over your life and your story up until this point. See what has served you until now. Should you continue on the path you are on? Or is it time to rewrite your story? While you still have time. It's not too late. Embrace the good and the necessary. Eliminate the rest. Remember, "To eat the fish and spit out the bones" You Too, Are Beautiful Beyond All Your Scars. "Trust God, No Matter What" End of Story!

BEAUTY BEYOND THE SCARS

Great Is Thy Mercy by Donnie McClurkin

Go listen to it now.

I bet you feel what I felt!

MY DAD'S FAMOUS SERMON

I've Seen Something That God Hasn't Seen

Many of us over our lifetime have encounter someone who was smarter than us, physically stronger than us, richer, and even wiser, creative, and more powerful than us and so on. However, as my dad brought to life in one of his famous sermons; that if you ask anyone still around today they remember him. They would tell you. That it was one of his most memorable. We may have seen and experienced several things, but God has never seen anyone, smarter, stronger, richer, wiser, creative, and more powerful than He. He Is Almighty! So when you've been a witness and really take the time to ponder on that in your heart. Just on things that God has done in your own life, you can agree that you have also seen something that God hasn't seen. So just embrace the fact that, if you "Trust Him, No Matter What." He always has your back. A few other sermons: that my dad wrote:

- He Is Almighty
- The World Series
- I Love You and There's Nothing You Can Do About It
- Shake, Rattle & Roll

SONGS THAT BROUGHT ME THROUGH 🎵

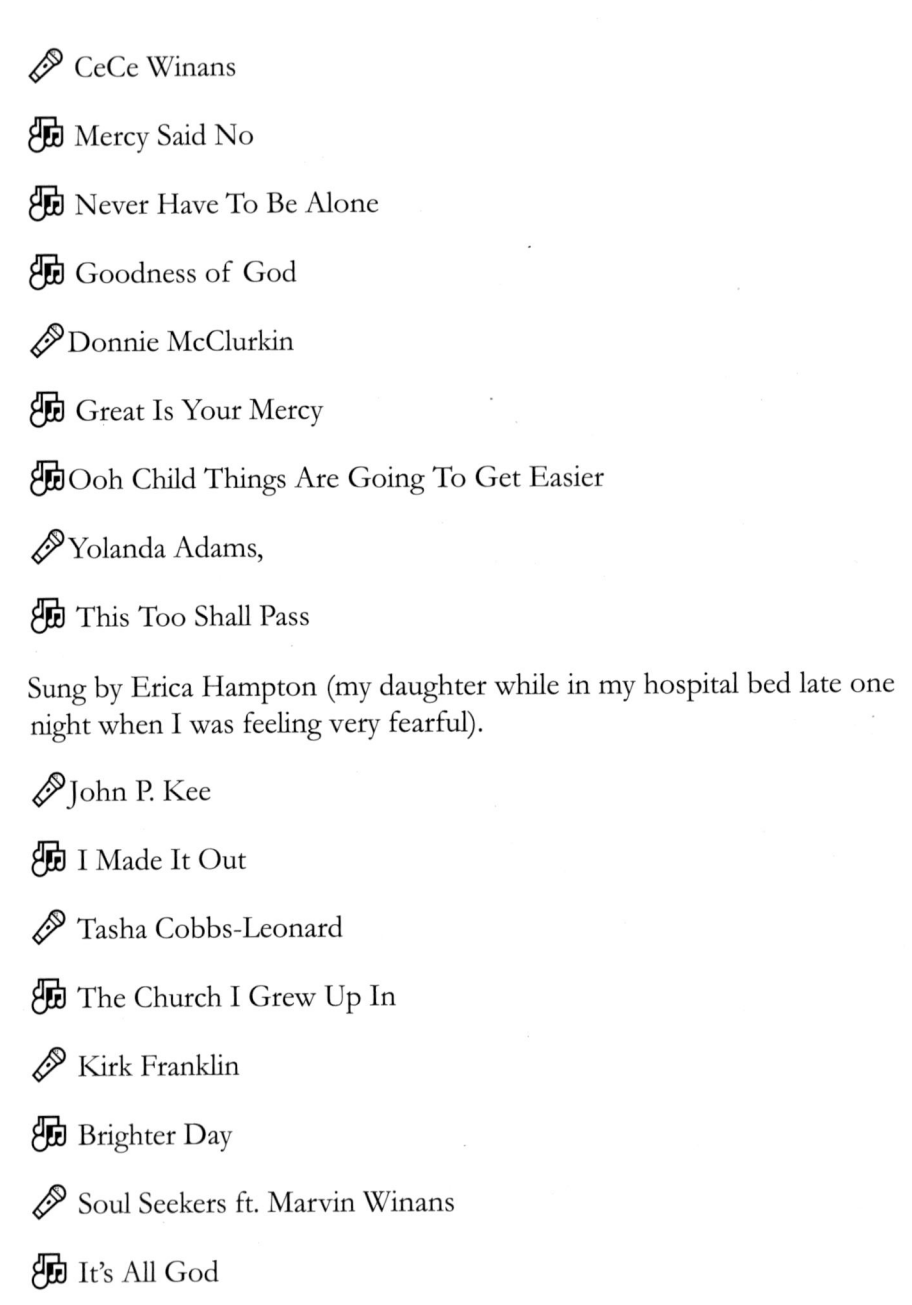

🎤 CeCe Winans

🎵 Mercy Said No

🎵 Never Have To Be Alone

🎵 Goodness of God

🎤 Donnie McClurkin

🎵 Great Is Your Mercy

🎵 Ooh Child Things Are Going To Get Easier

🎤 Yolanda Adams,

🎵 This Too Shall Pass

Sung by Erica Hampton (my daughter while in my hospital bed late one night when I was feeling very fearful).

🎤 John P. Kee

🎵 I Made It Out

🎤 Tasha Cobbs-Leonard

🎵 The Church I Grew Up In

🎤 Kirk Franklin

🎵 Brighter Day

🎤 Soul Seekers ft. Marvin Winans

🎵 It's All God

MY MOM'S SONGS

Trouble in my way I have to cry sometime... Jesus He will fix it...

What Is This... whatever it is it won't let me hold my peace.

Operator Long Distance Give Me Jesus On the Line.

I've got a feeling that everything is going to be alright!

Because He Lives, I Can face Tomorrow

MY FAMILY ALBUM

Paternal Great-grandmother and Paternal and Maternal Grandparents and Parents

Old Friends - Adrian & Zelda

Our Happily Ever After

The Lanes

Sugar and Spice

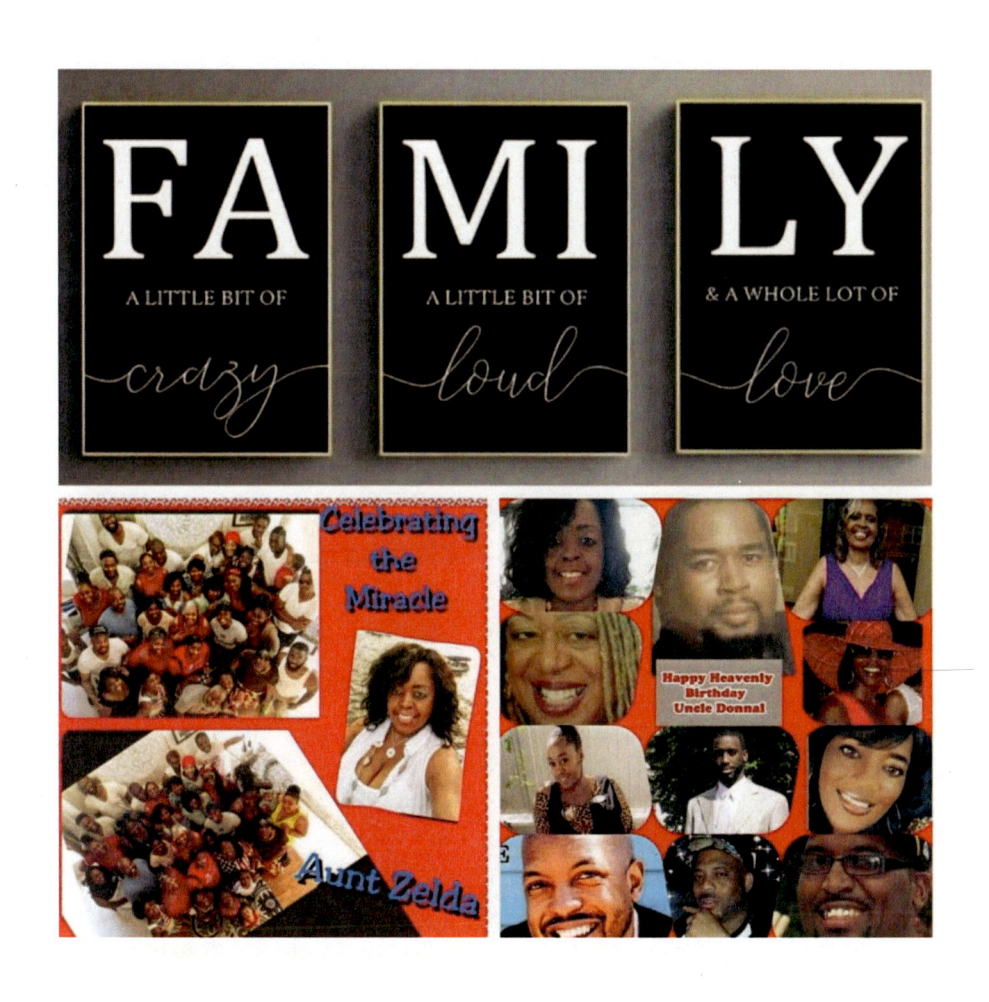

My FAMILY

Cousin Connections

First and Second Cousins

The Brother's Johnson with mom and dad

Friends Who Became Family

The Walls, The Bentleys, and The Johnsons

The A2Z Experience

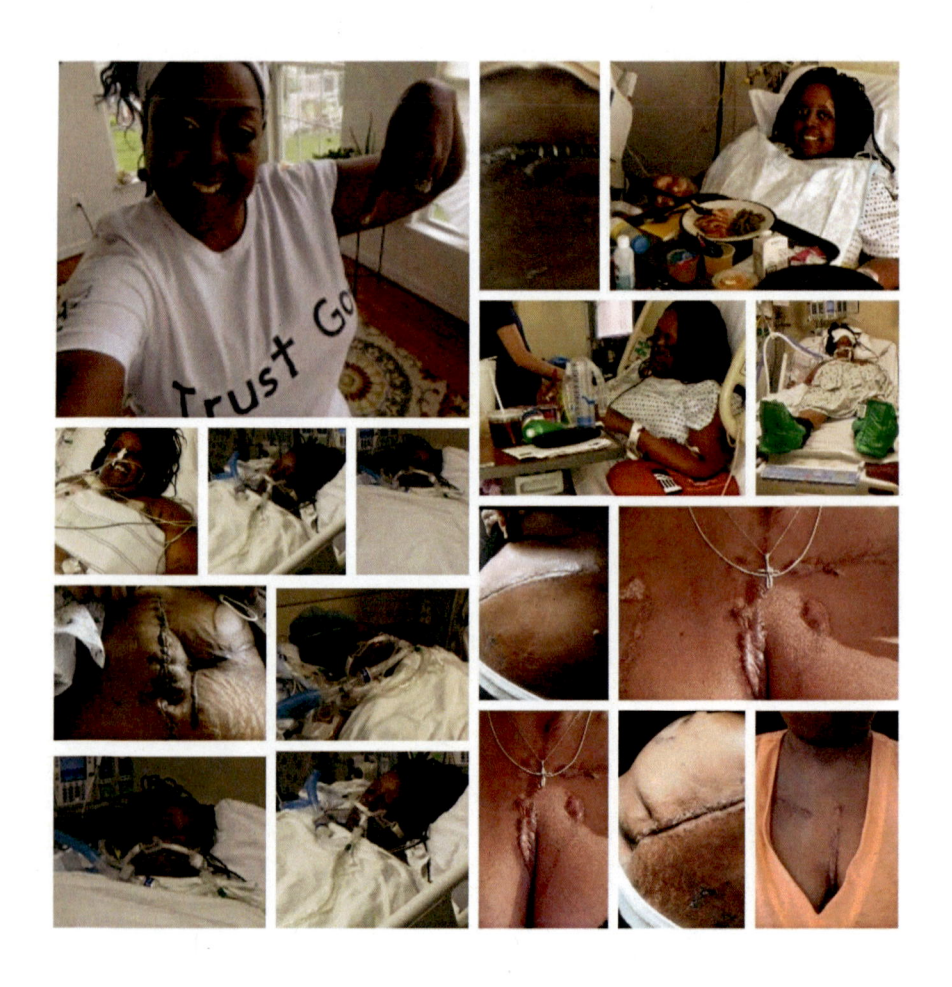

Beauty Beyond the Scars

Trust God No Matter What

SUGGESTED READINGS

The Message Bible and the Book of Proverbs

The 5 Love Languages
Gary Chapman

The Four Agreements
Don Miguel Ruiz

Why Christians Get Sick
Rev. George H. Malkmus

Standing On The Edge Of Your Tomorrow
Belinda Marie Lane

Life Interrupted- How Covid-19
Is Reshaping our Relationship with God, Health & Business
Dean Heath
Co Author- Zelda Johnson

SPEAKING ENGAGEMENTS AND BOOKINGS

To book Zelda D. Johnson for your next conference or in-house event, please contact her at zstyle14@yahoo.com.

ORGANIZATIONS and CORPORATIONS

This book is available at special quantity discounts for bulk purchases. This book is perfect for employee gifts, sales promotions, premiums, or fund-raising. Give the gift of *Beauty Beyond the Scars: A Second Chance at Life...A Second Chance at Love.*

To order copies 1-1000

https://linktr.ee/a2zexperience2014
(717)347-8618

Zelda D. Johnson

THE A2Z EXPERIENCE

MISSION:

Our Goal Is To Make A Statement As Well As A Lasting Impact As We Love Life And Each Other. We Are Inspiring Others "To Trust God No Matter What" While Having An A2ZExperience.

HISTORY:

Est:1979-1981-2010-2017 (Bonded)

GOALS:

To Love God, Life, and Each Other

SERVICES:

Seminars and Speaking Engagements

- Health and Wealth
- Financial Education
- Entertainment Productions
- Jewelry/Brooches
- Savings Banks
- Inspirational Messages
- Books
- Bags
- Mugs

DEDICATED ORGANIZATIONS

I wish to personally thank the persons who represent the organizations below. (A brief description of each one is listed below).

♡   American Heart Association

Website: heart.org

Renne Sattiewhite, President and Chief Executive Officer

(CEO) African American Credit Union Coalition (AACUC)

Website: aacuc.org

Toinette Shearer (Owner/Director)

Center for Hope & Healing,

Website: centerforhopeandhealing.net

Crystal Jewelz (Founder/CEO)

Jewelz Connect 3.0

Jewelzinc17@gmail.com

704-625-6519

https://linktr.ee/Jewelzconnect

Belinda M. Lane

Friday at Sundown, (Author/Speaker)

Website: fridayatsundown4@gmail.com

Michele Ellis-Williams (Founder/CEO)

Homecare Coaching and Consulting,

Website: coachmichelewilliams.com

Juanita Collick

The L.A.W. Character and Etiquette Program V, Inc. (The L.A.W. Program)

Email: setmeup2learn@gmail.com

Erica Victoria (Singer/Artist/Entertainer)

Lyrically Sound Entertainment

Email: ericavictoriamusic@gmail.com

Diane P. Belton

To God Be the Glory, (Speaker/Woman of God)

Email: toGodbetheglory52@gmail.com

BIBLICAL SCRIPTURES

Be Intentional About the Life You Want to Create!

These were the scriptures that helped me the most during my life's journey. I pray that you will find strength in these passages as well.

Delight thyself also in the LORD; and he shall give thee the desires of thine heart.

Psalms 37:4

For the LORD God is a sun and shield: the LORD will give grace and glory: no good thing will he withhold from them that walk uprightly.

Psalms 84:11

Verily, Verily I Say Unto You, He That Believeth On Me, The Works That I Do Shall He Do Also; And Greater Works Than These Shall He Do; Because I Go Unto My Father.

John 14:12 (KJV)

Trust in the Lord with all thine heart; and lean not unto thine own understanding. In all thy ways acknowledge Him, and He shall direct thy paths.

Proverbs 3:5

Now unto him that is able to do exceeding Abundantly above all that we ask or think, according to the power that workers in us.

Ephesians 3:2

For I will restore health unto thee, and I will heal thee of thy wounds, sayeth the Lord

Jeremiah 30:17

AFFIRMATIONS FROM THE HEART!

"Our greatest weakness lies in giving up. The most certain way to succeed is always just try one more time".

Thomas Edison

"You're braver than you believe. Stronger than you see, and smarter than you think."

A.A. Milne

"When you change the way you look at things, the things you look at change."

Wayne Dyer

"Life is not measured by the number of breath we take but by the moments that take our breath away."

Maya Angelou

"I already know what giving up feels like. I want to see what happens if I don't."

Neila Rey

"Live the life that you imagine. Give your dreams a place to live."

Zelda D. Johnson

"Enjoy Your Day. Enjoy Your Life. Enjoy Each Other. Enjoy Each Experience."

Zelda D. Johnson

"Broken Crayons Still Color."

Rahil Khan

"Today is the opportunity to build the tomorrow you want."

Myron Golden

"You don't need a good idea; you need a God idea."

Myron Golden

"You were born to win, but to be a winner you must plan to win. Prepare to win and expect to win!"

Zig Ziglar

"Time is up when your heart stops, as long as you have a beat in your heart, it's time to make your wildest dreams come true."

Taraji P. Henson